Thank goodness, there's more than one life to live !

J. Michael Surkamp MBE

Thank goodness, there's more than one life to live !

True personal experiences by people who have overcome all doubt in repeated lives on earth!

J. Michael Surkamp MBE

Thank goodness, there's more than one life!

True personal experiences by people who have over-come all doubt in repeated lives on earth!

1ˢᵗ edition published by:
Author House UK ᴸᵗᵈ ISBN 978-1-4389-0865-6

New revised edition ISBN 978-0-9569266-0-9

This publication © Anastasi ᴸᵗᵈ· 2011
Published by:
Anastasi ᴸᵗᵈ·, 152 Godiva Road, Leominster, Herefordshire UK

A catalogue record for this book is available from the British Library

Book and Cover design by: © Anastasi ᴸᵗᵈ· Design Studio 2011
Typeset in Adobe Garamond Pro by Anastasi ᴸᵗᵈ·
Printed and Bound by
Lightning Source UKᴸᵗᵈ·

Dedication

I would like to dedicate the book to Thomas H. Meyer, author of 'Rudolf Steiner's Core Mission' and 'Light for the new Millennium'.

Contents

d next line, continue with: 'one thing...'
6.

e

r Johnson, pg 176, should be omitted.

ence accepted with thanks. *(to publisher)*

'so little of what Rudolf Steiner has

ERRATA

Numbers refer to pages.

26: after ...'doctrine is' - omit rest of line an
39: 1812 is correct. The person died in 182
66: omit 3+ lines after 'wallet'
135 : (I give the correct spelling only:) Cayc
147: Although at
153: dumbfounded
156: there ran
156: resistance
157: extension
162: this is correct - The last paragraph af
164: animosity
169: and then it...
176: omit passage after Johnson
176: murmured
184: 0mit 'd' after Meyer
194: Your proposal for re-arrangement of s
195: summary
199: thought
200: worlds
204: 1966 is correct
208: omit second 'that'
214: summary
218 and 224: 1966 - also add 'of ' in senten
239: dimensions
245: Century

Foreword

In this book I want to acknowledge some out-standing pioneers in the study of Reincarnation and Karma – the re-embodiment of the spirit, and the acceptance of the lawful consequences of deeds done in former lives. They have contributed to a change of consciousness which, I feel, would be a vital healing factor in our time. The truth of repeated lives on earth is still relegated to the area of personal beliefs, to the paranormal, to psychological phenomena, or to sensational entertainment. Because it relies initially on subjective intuition, there is still a wide gulf between this form of recognition and the objective methods of natural science. In the East the ideas of reincarnation and karma are culturally alive through tradition, though in the form of the migration of souls, or metempsychosis, whereas in the West the idea was suppressed by the Christian Church. It was during the Age of Enlightenment that individual thinkers, poets and philosophers came to their considered conclusion that the idea of reincarnation and karma was the only rational answer to the puzzle of human life. Those men who had the courage to disagree with dogma and the ruling powers were named as heretics and ostracised, or burned at the stake. Later on they had to guard themselves against being ridiculed. This was the case with the German philosopher and playwright Gotthold Ephraim Lessing (1729-1781), who had to publish his treatise on 'The Education of the Human Race' under a pseudonym. In this essay he describes how in ancient and pre-Christian times men had to be led like children under the strict authority of tribal and religious leaders. Only in stages, which he compares to school classes, did individual faculties evolve, and gradually emancipation from dogma and tutelage took place. For Lessing, the only fitting thought was that individuals must have advanced through this school of history by returning to life again and again. Blind faith was to be replaced by knowledge and the certainty of a higher self with direct access to powers divine. The downside of this development (the shift in consciousness during the Enlightenment) was the emergence of a reliance on the human intellect alone and the acknowledgement only of the visible world; this led mankind into the trap of materialism. The increasing experience and acceptance of the idea of repeated lives on earth in our time is a ray of hope for a sea change of consciousness, to include the vital spiritual factor that is dormant in every individual human being.

What in the eighteenth and nineteenth centuries were only tender shoots has developed strong fibres during the first half of the twentieth century via dreams, psychometry, far-memory and spontaneous memories by children. During the first quarter of that century, Rudolf Steiner researched the realm of spirit and developed his Spiritual Science, which gives cogent insights into the workings of karma and reincarnation. He was convinced that our time is in need of this knowledge and that it should spread, even before it was scientifically proven – as did the 'heliocentric' Copernican system, with the Sun rather than the Earth being at the centre of the Universe, in the sixteenth century. In the second half of the twentieth century, scientists, working with or without hypnosis, 'discovered' reincarnation empirically and now a number of psychologists work successfully as past-life therapists.

The appreciation of the truth of repeated earth-lives and the sojourn of soul and spirit in the spirit world during the intervals will forever be an answer to the riddles of life, to social and political questions, to personal spiritual development and to a truthful extension of science with a peaceful and compassionate application of technology. Moreover, this truth, sensibly introduced to school pupils at an appropriate age, would have a strong impact on their mental development and their outlook on life and society and would, I believe, strengthen the moral sense of responsibility of young persons towards themselves, others and the environment.

J. Michael Surkamp

A CREED

I held that when a person dies
His soul returns again to earth;
Arrayed in some new flesh-disguise
Another mother gives him birth.
With sturdier limbs and brighter brain
The old soul takes the road again.

Such was my own belief and trust;
This hand, this hand that holds the pen,
Has many a hundred times been dust,
And turned, as dust, to dust again;
These eyes of mine have blinked and shone
In Thebes, in Troy, in Babylon.

All that I rightly think or do,
Or make, or spoil, or bless, or blast,
Is curse or blessing justly due
For sloth or effort in the past.
My life's a statement of the sum
Of vice indulged, or overcome.

I know that in my lives to be
My sorry heart will ache and burn,
And worship unavailingly,
The woman whom I used to spurn,
And shake to see another have
The love I spurned, the love she gave.

And shall I know, in angry words,
In gibes and mocks, and many a tear,
A carrion flock of homing-birds,
The gibes and scorns I uttered here,
The brave word that I failed to speak
Will brand me dastard on the cheek.

And as I wander on the roads
I shall be helped and healed and blessed;
Dear words shall cheer and be as goads
To urge to heights before unguessed.
My road shall be the road I made;
All that I gave shall be repaid.

So shall I fight, so shall I tread,
In this long war beneath the stars;
So shall a glory wreath my head,
So shall I faint and show the scars,
Until this case, this clogging mould,
Be smithied all to kingly gold.

John Masefield.

Thank goodness there is more than one life to live !

"Death used to be human-scale. People generally died at home, within a family or community or society within which death was a normal occurrence and where, despite the loss, there was comfort in a shared religious belief in an afterlife. If death occurred in war, it was again human-sized: largely in man-to-man conflict. With the advent of mechanised war, and perhaps especially in our own time with the use of highly sophisticated, remote and often indiscriminate weapons capable of mass killing, and with the widespread erosion of religious faith, the questions surrounding death – is there an afterlife? is there a judgement? – have become more pointed. We value our own life and manner of death and would prefer our death to be dignified, painless and timely" (Paul Carline), but what about the tens and hundreds of thousands, even millions, of people for whose deaths we are co-responsible? In the course of the two Great Wars, the atrocities and accidents caused by human error of the last century and on into this present one, more than a hundred million human lives have been snuffed out, sometimes in an instant, sometimes after long suffering. Do we think to ask where are the souls and spirits of those who have died? Does it occur to us that they are bound to come again, the vanquished and the victims as also the victors and the perpetrators!

When will the vicious circle of violence end? This will depend on each living human being changing their ideas (re-thinking, the real meaning of "repent") resulting in a sea change of attitude similar to our new relationship to the natural world. Our dependence on the 'natural environment' has been recognised and now it is up to us to recognise the equally important dependence on a 'spiritual environment'– where the souls live when their bodies have been destroyed (for a while after death, whether natural or violent). They will come again, graced with new innocence and hopeful of bettering the world we live in. Are we to disappoint them and burden them with outdated slogans like 'survival of the fittest', or false dogmas of the supremacy of matter, and teach them that might equals right and that selfishness, greed and group egotism is all that counts?

The dawning of a New Age is in evidence and positive news is spreading. The night has to give way to a new day, a Sun-Day, of mankind.

This book has called on witnesses of the eternal truth of repeated lives on earth and the destiny we share as members of the human race. For some it will be a wake-up call and an end to denial; for others it will be a confirmation that a world of the spirit exists which is our home and from which we come again and again in order to develop the sort of freedom which takes responsibility and cares for those more vulnerable than ourselves and for our total environment. This is no utopia, but a new orientation and a new path to follow.

Chapter 1

What scientists discover through regression

Five researchers are presented in this first chapter, all of whom intentionally set out to justify to the demands of scientific discipline and the scientific establishment every step they have taken in their research. All of them worked with hypnosis and made unexpected discoveries which had to be justified by reference to their own critical rationality and scientific conscience. In pursuit of their project, each of them had to acknowledge that an element of 'chance' played an important role in making their particular 'discovery.' The writer himself bases his own conviction regarding reincarnation and karma on the proof his long life has given him of the truth which he experienced in the writings and printed lectures of Rudolf Steiner. Although he does not advocate hypnosis as a tool for research, he acknowledges its widespread use and therapeutic benefit to certain patients when applied conscientiously. The examples given by the following scientists follow a certain progression. Denys Kelsey discovered that part in the human soul which seemed able to incarnate; Thorwald Dethlefsen showed that regression under psychotherapy always leads to definite former persona; Roger Woolger also made the chance discovery of reincarnation when engaging in Jungian psychotherapy; Joel Whitton established empirically the existence of an interval between incarnations, and Helen Wambach confirmed through her group regressions the existence of memories from the time before birth. Each of these scientists drew their own conclusions, which differed in parts, but were in overall agreement through the results of their research with the facts of reincarnation, karma and the existence of a period between death and birth.

Dr Denys Kelsey – discovers in the Unconscious what can reincarnate

Denys Kelsey, MD, M.R.C.P made an important discovery in the realm of the unconscious. In dealing with one of his patients under hypnosis, he came 'face to face' with that entity within the unconscious which he recognised as the individuality, mysteriously hidden, with the potential to reincarnate. He 'discovered' that part of the human being which incarnates!

He also asks questions about the barrier protecting this realm. Although all therapists who use hypnosis find it essential to gain access to and extract knowledge from the unconscious, his questions about the barrier were vague; he even considered the possibility that the barrier might be formed chemically or electrically. Undoubtedly, healing benefits arise by penetrating into the unconscious and allowing the patient to relive experiences which had become blockages or neuroses; this is self-evident. On the other hand, it is also true that it is of great benefit to us that the barrier exists and that a kind of amnesia- a forgetting – throws a veil over past experiences; how else could we meet the new challenges of this present life without prejudice!

The best introduction to Denys Kelsey probably comes from the book "Many Lifetimes" which he co-authored with Joan Grant,.The following quote is taken from Chapter Two, entitled: "Recognition of Reality":

"I should like people to share my belief in reincarnation; I think it would cause them to be much happier, much less frightened, and very much more sane. For a psychiatrist to hold this belief and to have made it the basis of his therapy is still rather unusual. It is not a belief which I have always held, so I will begin by explaining how I was led to it by clinical evidence which had been accumulating during the ten years before I learned that somebody called Joan Grant was able to remember many of her earlier lives. Without this work I would not have been able so rapidly to appreciate the value of what Joan was able to contribute; because, like so many people, I cannot accept a concept unless it satisfies my intellect and relates to my empirical experience.

I was precipitated into the practice of psychiatry, at the age of thirty-one, without even an hour's warning. In this I was fortunate; it meant that I approached the subject without any preconceived ideas, for when I was a medical student, psychiatry played only a very small part in the curriculum. I remember that I was taught that the causes of thyrotoxicosis were "sex sepsis and psychic trauma"; and I attended a series of lecture-demonstrations, but rather lightheartedly, because questions on psychiatry never occurred in the examinations. And that, to the best of my recollection, was that!

But immediately upon embarking on

psychiatry, a series of cases came my way which, step by step, extended the framework of what I believed to be fact until, after four years, a session with a particular patient forced me to the intellectual certainty that in a human being there is a component that is not physical. To be taught this as a matter of dogma or doctrine is when their bodies have been destroyed [for a while after death, whether natural or violent]. one thing; to be compelled to the same conclusion by one's own experience is quite another. I did not realise it at the time, but this session was an important landmark on the way to a belief in reincarnation; at least I had got so far as believing in the reality of something which could reincarnate!"

In 1948 Kelsey was working on the medical side of a large military hospital, a post which he owed to the fact that three years previously he had passed the postgraduate examination which is the start of a long road to recognition as a consulting physician or intern. He was still travelling on that road when an epidemic of influenza hit the hospital and abruptly changed his course. One of the first casualties was a medical officer in the psychiatric wing and Kelsey was asked, temporarily, to take on as much of this work as he could. Late that night he learned that he had an aptitude for inducing hypnosis.

He was summoned urgently to the ward to give a sedative injection to a patient who had suddenly become acutely disturbed and violent. By the time he arrived, three muscular orderlies had the situation under control and were holding the patient firmly down on his bed. He had the feeling that the man was unlikely to resume his violence, so he motioned the orderlies to leave. But the patient was obviously still very frightened, and with no intention beyond trying to calm his fears, he sat down beside him and began to talk to him in what he hoped was a soothing and reassuring voice. Kelsey certainly did not realise that he then began to use one of the standard techniques for inducing hypnosis. It had simply occurred to him that if he could get the patient to fix his attention on something outside himself, he might be less disturbed by his ideas and feelings, so Kelsey asked him to fix his gaze on a dim light on the ceiling above his head. For the same reason he also coaxed him to concentrate upon his breathing, making it perfectly regular and rhythmical, but a little slower and a little deeper than usual.

The patient was still very tense. His fists were tightly clenched and his arms and legs showed a fine tremor. So Kelsey drew his attention to each of his limbs in turn, urging him to relax them and to allow them to remain relaxed. These instructions were interspersed with assurances that he had nothing to fight, nothing to fear. Gradually he became perceptibly calmer, until he was lying completely relaxed. Purely for good measure, Kelsey continued talking to him in the same vein and he recalls suggesting to him, quite casually, that he might as well go off to sleep. At this, the patient's eyes rolled up and his eyelids came down in a curiously positive way and suddenly Kelsey realised to his astonishment that he must have hypnotised him!

The next morning Kelsey described the incident to the psychiatrist in charge of the department, who confirmed that this was almost certainly what had happened. He was equally intrigued and asked Kelsey to repeat the technique on another patient, a man who was suffering from neurosis as a result of a horrific accident with an automobile. This patient entered hypnosis very quickly, and with a tremendous release of emotion relived the circumstances of the accident. The psychiatrist assured him that it would be a simple matter to clear up the residue of the neurosis. During the next few weeks Kelsey was able to treat several other patients in a similar way; they too relived the relevant episodes with great release of emotion and went on to make a rapid recovery. He found these experiences in the military hospital so rewarding that he decided henceforth to specialise in psychiatry. Once back in civil life, he took a post in a mental hospital where he remained for the next six years.

Kelsey goes on to explain his experiences with hypnosis:

"Hypnosis has played such a large part in the experiences I had that I shall shortly say something about it. A convenient starting point is the widely accepted concept that there are three distinct compartments of mental activity. First there is the compartment of consciousness to which I shall usually refer as 'normal-waking-consciousness'. This contains only the thoughts and sensations of which we are aware at any present moment. Next, there is the compartment known as the 'pre-conscious'. Here is stored every memory, every item of knowledge, that can be summoned to consciousness at will. Thirdly, there is the compartment with which a psychiatrist tends to be especially concerned and which is usually called 'the unconscious'.

The contents of this compartment lie behind a barrier, the precise nature of which is not known. It may prove to be essentially chemical, electrical, or even purely psychological, but whatever its nature may prove to be, the effect is that material that lies behind the barrier can be brought across it into normal waking-consciousness only with considerable difficulty.

Hypnosis is sometimes loosely spoken of as sleep, but this is inaccurate. Indeed, unless a specific suggestion is made to the contrary, a person under hypnosis may be unusually wide-awake, in the sense that his powers of perception may be abnormally acute. But since such a person is not in a state of normal waking-consciousness, perhaps the best description of hypnosis is 'a state of altered consciousness'. This can be of particular value to psychiatry because it may enable the therapist to bring material from the patient's unconscious to the surface much more quickly than would otherwise be possible.

I have always considered myself fortunate in that, at a very early stage, I encountered a patient who illustrated the reality of the unconscious, and the power of material held in that compartment, in an unforgettable way.

The patient was a young woman who was wheeled into the ward in a chair because she had lost the use of her legs. A few days previously she had awakened in the morning to find that they were completely paralysed. Examination showed that there was nothing wrong with the nerves or muscles or bones, and that this was a paralysis of psychological origin.

In conversation she was clear-headed, calm and indeed rather cheerful: surprisingly so for someone who, on the face of it, might never be able to use her legs again. We discussed many details of her life, including the fact that since her marriage she had become very disillusioned about her husband. However, the previous year life had not been too bad because he had been abroad on business. Then, almost casually, she mentioned that a few days before the paralysis occurred, she had received a letter, which made her feel obliged to join him. She admitted that she was 'a bit scared' at the prospect, but her principles demanded that nonetheless she should go. She added that her parents would be terribly distressed to learn that all was not well between her husband and herself.

Her voice had been level and matter-of-fact as she was telling me this. There was nothing to suggest a young woman striving to speak coherently while in a state of acute fear. But under hypnosis, when I brought the conversation round to her forthcoming trip, a very different picture emerged. She was not simply 'a bit scared': she was terrified! And as details of conditions she expected to find at the end of her journey also emerged, her fear was understandable. She was weeping and trembling, but through her sobs I heard her exclaim, 'I would rather have no legs than have to go!'

I then brought her slowly back to normal waking-consciousness, insisting as I did so that she remember all she had been telling me. Now that the full extent of her fear was in consciousness, she was scarcely recognisable as the poised young woman who had been wheeled into the ward. But now her problems were where we could explore them and cut them down to size.

We were able to discuss in exactly what respect her parents would be distressed to learn the true state of affairs, and it was not difficult to get her to consider rationally whether it was really necessary to stay with her husband. I was able to remind her that she was able to earn her living before her marriage and could easily do so again. By the end of this session she was very much calmer and already had some power of movement in her legs.

During the next few days we had further talks along similar lines. Suddenly she declared that she had realised the significance of the paralysis of her legs. It was the only way she could avoid joining her husband without feeling that she was betraying what had been her principles. Within days after this session her legs were functioning perfectly normally."

Several others followed this case history: each bore witness to Kelsey having recognised a reality hitherto obscured to him.

To the discussion of intrauterine consciousness he adds important findings: "I asked her to go even further back to a time when she felt the same tone of emotion. She said, 'I am very tiny. I seem to be lying on something very soft and white. I am very comfort-able but somehow it is not right. I used to be part of a 'oneness' but now I am separated.' At this I told her that at the count of ten she would find herself again part of the 'oneness'. As I reached 'ten' she said, quietly and positively, 'this is the womb'. She went on: 'there is something beating in me – my mother's heart. I can't see – and it feels as if I have got no mouth'. I asked her in what position she found herself. She replied 'curled up', and immediately assumed the posture of a foetus.

As she seemed to be perfectly comfortable, I left a nurse with her and went to fetch the medical superintendent to see this interesting phenomenon. While he watched, I told her that at the count of ten she would start to leave this place. At 'ten' she arched her back, put one hand on her head, and an expression of severe suffering appeared on her features. She was portraying exactly what one can imagine a baby feels when the first contractions of the uterus clamp down upon it. In a moment or two this attitude was relaxed, only to be repeated some minutes later."

Later, Denys Kelsey drew the following conclusion: "I also gained reason to believe that from at least as early as the fifth month of intra-uterine life the unborn baby is aware of itself as an individual. It is aware of its sex, of its position, of the length of time it has been in the womb, and of the relationship of its limbs to one another. One patient, who had a most difficult birth, regressed to a period which he positively stated was the fifth month of intra-uterine life. He was aware that the cord had become wound round his neck and also that his right arm had become trapped beneath his right leg. I have no obstetrical records to confirm this, but it would account most adequately for the difficulty experienced in delivering him. I remained puzzled by the fact that patients often dated memorable intra-uterine events so positively until, ten years later, Joan offered what I think is the correct explanation: a mother is usually very conscious of the precise stage of her pregnancy, and the foetus picks this up by telepathy."

The partnership of Denys Kelsey and Joan Grant has helped clarify many issues and has increased Kelsey's healing potential.

Thorwald Dethlefsen – discovers reincarnation (De)

Thorwald Dethlefsen is a practising psychologist, past-life therapist and writer in Munich, Germany. He presents his work as a scientist working on the basis of repeatable experiments. He regressed his subjects beyond birth, enquired about the prenatal experience and finally asked what went before that. In protocols taken of the questions asked, as well as the answers given by his subjects, he came to the firm conclusion that he was able to prove the existence of former lives – scientifically.

He was surprised, whilst researching the question of intra-uterine life and what went before, when his subject made a reference to a former life. He had 'discovered' reincarnation empirically and 'by accident'. He then repeated the 'experiment', proving it to be scientifically verifiable. This led him to follow up his first discovery with many other subjects. Any lingering doubts were dissolved by the wealth of material that he accumulated over the years in his practice in Munich. The past-life case histories he presented are impressive! The records are held in his archives in Munich. It is significant that after his discovery, Dethlefsen became a past-life therapist and healer.

The following passages explain his starting point:

"It is now just seven years since, in 1968, I conducted an experiment for the first time which not only became the basis and starting point for my later work of research but also for my view of the world. Of all this I did not have any idea when I demonstrated in front of an interested circle of lay people some hypnotic experiments. After my 'medium' (the usual, somewhat unhappy terminology for the hypnotized person) experienced through me his forgotten past and some episodes from his childhood, I tried to find out whether it was possible for him to remember, and even experience, his own birth. The experiment succeeded. My medium, an engineer of around 25 years, started with sighing and changed his breathing rhythm and described the process of his birth. This surprising success encouraged me to probe further back in time. I suggested to him that he was in his mother's womb three months before his birth. Immediately he started to tell about his impressions as an embryo. Yet this evening I wanted to know more. 'We go now still further back – so far back until you hit on some event which you can describe clearly…' A suspended silence came about, my medium breathed heavily, then began speaking with a muffled voice. He told of his perceptions; and when I questioned him further – the story of a man took shape, by name of Guy Lafarge, born in 1852, who lived in the Alsace, sold vegetables and finally died as a stable-hand in 1880. Finally I returned him to 'this' life and woke him up. …"

"With my first experiment I still had the feeling that I had succeeded with something truly exceptional and sensational; a mixture of awe and anxiety prevented me from repeating the experiment more frequently. I only dared to make the step beyond birth with people who had entered a deep trance; I experienced trepidation of the new and unknown. I also had a certain anxiety when meeting phases such as illness, accidents and death and quickly swerved from traumatic events and returned my medium back into 'this' life. ... and was relieved that all had gone well when my medium smiled happily without knowing what he had experienced and told during the session. During the intervening time much, even everything, has changed fundamentally. Anxiety was replaced by experience, uncertainty by detailed knowledge of the processes. What years ago was an event for me, has now become my daily work. ... This has been achieved by a considerable improvement in the regression-technique which is now so refined that I find the 'entrance' with almost every person."

Based on this practical experience and also by reference to Eastern philosophy, Dethlefsen became convinced of the fact of former earth-lives. Some of the other conclusions he came to are not shared by other researchers. One concerns the nature of the law of karma. He rebukes those who disagree with fatalism and determinism and advocates voluntary subjugation to the karmic law by recognising 'that man owns only one single freedom, that is, to believe himself to be free.' In this, we could say that his interpretation is pre-Christian and rather in tune with the Muslim faith of total subjugation to fate. His demand for 'complete self-recognition' fails to recognise the difference between the total 'subjugation' of his 'research-subjects' and of himself as the initiator of the research, and the freedom he takes in applying his skills.

After having established the 'scientific proof' of the reincarnation of an individual, Dethlefsen now devotes himself to psychotherapy in tandem with past-life therapy. The book makes no reference to the fact that this knowledge and practice is also applied in other countries, as the cases of Joel L Whitton and Denys Kelsey, Roger Woolger and Arnall Bloxham illustrate.

The special value of Dethlefsen's book lies in the verbatim protocols of a number of regressions. Like all past-life therapists, he focuses on psychological block-ages and phobias, which cannot be explained by present life experiences, nor healed by conventional means. He realises that doctors and psychologists can only provide insights and suggestions, yet the patient has to follow this up with an actual deed. The very revisiting of situations and reliving of past traumas is often enough for the patient to come to terms in his day-consciousness with a past event and to kindle the will to make amends for whatever in his or her own past life actions was the root cause. This process demands of the hypnotist to quasi play the role of a priest, withholding all moral judgement and accepting 'confessions' from the individual's former persona – from beyond the grave, as it were.

Dethlefsen poses the question of what meaning and value it will have for those persons among the billions of human beings living on earth to be 'cata-pulted' into the insights of their own past. He finds the answer in the concept of 'karma', which entails that a problem has to be met again and again until it is seen as an opportunity for making amends. By taking this into account he firmly supports the idea of development as a spiritual or consciousness evolu-tion. He quotes the saying from Matthew 5 in the New Testament: 'Therefore you shall be perfect, just as your Father in heaven is perfect'.

Dethlefsen mentions that in the Second Council of Constantinople in 553 CE Reincarnation as a belief system was removed from our Western thinking . The argument was actually against the Doctrine of the Pre-existence of the Soul. Interestingly the early Christian Fathers stated these beliefs. Justin Martyr (100 – 165 CE) said the soul inhabits the human body more than once and denied that the embodied form could remember previous experiences. Origen (185 – 254 CE) stated: The soul, which is immaterial and invisible in its nature, exists in no material place without having a body suited to the nature of that place. Accordingly, it at one time puts off one body, which was necessary before, but which is no longer adequate in its changed state and it exchanges it for a second. He does not ask why this was done.

Might it have been that direct spiritual experiences and memories had diminished and only superstition was left? Was it done in order to emphasise the uniting of the individual soul with the entirely unique event of Christ's incarnation?

Another significant realisation came from many answers his subjects have given concerning their own experiences during their embryonic state and the birth process. His findings contradict current assumptions that during this period no consciousness exists. Several of his subjects were able to recall events during and after birth, even reporting the presence of persons, the bright light and loud sounds and the meaning of what was spoken! Some of the subjects acted out strong emotions in reliving their birth-experience. This knowledge could have an impact on practices in maternity hospitals and the handling of the newborn infant. What the doctor and midwife say, or even think, is remembered in the deeper layers of the soul! A gentle approach in subdued light, a homely atmosphere instead of a clinical one, could be the rational outcome. It could also have a great bearing on the question of abortion. This might be an 'uncomfortable truth', but could usher in, beneficially, a new awareness.

To the question of population increase, Dethlefsen answers very plausibly: in our time the span between incarnations has shortened considerably. Our fast moving time seems to attract many more souls.

Dethlefson's research into the time between lives fails to mention the results of research by other past-life psychologists. His findings describe the human ego being left very much to itself in a rather dark, lonely environment to relive past-life experiences before being 'sucked in' and drawn into a new incarnation. He concludes that there are no meetings with former friends and relatives.

The Claudia Case (excerpts) is an example:

Dethlevsen begins his 40-page transcription of this session by saying, after the hypnotic state had been reached:

"Now we will go back in your life [that of a middle-aged woman] – Time is for us only a means of communication, a measurement – yet you will experience the past in such a way as it just happens this moment. – Past becomes present. – We go back in your life. You will become younger, your age is now 25 years. – We step back, now you are 15. Today is your tenth birthday; how are you?

Claudia: (C) Nothing special

Dethlevsen (D) Why not?

C: I have the flu

D: Did you get presents?

In a kind of cross-examination D inquires into all the circumstances. C is in a hospital. The nurse takes away her presents and gives it to other girls. D regresses her to her birth, establishes date (12.09.1812) and time and the fact that she had a caesarian delivery. She described all her in utero sensations of warmth, comfort and her mothers movements. All of it expressed very personally and unexpected. C was born illegitimate, the father a Baron, the mother a servant. There was a sister, two years and a half older. Secrecy had to be observed. She called her dad 'Papa' only when alone with him, otherwise the Lord. Papa had promised her a visit to Berlin where she wanted to see the King. In this episode D put her to the test by asking

D: In what vehicle do you travel, is it a big auto? She answers: Pardon, what are you saying?

D: Is it a big car or a bus?

C: Heavens, a what? We just travel in a horse-drawn coach, I have told you already.

D: With a horse-drawn coach?

C: Yes.

D: How many horses are pulling it?

C: Four.

D: Good, now we arrive in Berlin; tell me what happens next.

C Then describes the encounter with the King's entourage. She tells of the cold and how Papa wrapped her in his cloak. Then the king appears in his coach.

C: Ba, there was no need to see him; he is really odd and ugly; I had always thought a king to be beautiful and young – but that one, he is odd and I am disappointed.

D: Is his queen with him?

C: No, she has died – she is dead a long time – Papa – the Lord said – before I was born.

D: So you don't like the King?

C: No.

D: What does he look like?

C: Och, he is – ba – he is old, he is odd – he has so – I don't know, such a – that runs from his mouth back to his neck and he has quite a big nose (laughing) but Papa says one should not laugh about a King …

After a longer conversation D Regresses C back to the previous life. She was then the wife of a charcoal-burner and outlaw living in the Blackforest. Because of him she suffered the end of her life in a dungeon , plagued by rats. Her year of birth was 1697. She is speaking in broad Swabian dialect, telling of her persecution and the hunger she and her two small boys suffer. D inquires about her feelings when caught and thrown in the dungeon. She has died of hunger. Now her body has no feelings; she is aware of the rats and the guards roughly ascertaining that she is dead.

Then D continues: Good – what follows then?

C: Yes, I can see and perceive everything, but I am everywhere and nowhere – you know this is a state – how shall I explain – so – everything is in balance and quiet and you can wish where you want to be – and then you are there at once you are there suddenly – simply by thoughts – because you have no body anymore.

D: Do you want to have one again? A body?

C: No, if it goes the same way again, no, I don't think so, if such a thing should happen again as that which had just happened, no, no, I don't want another body!

D: Do you always remain in that state?

C: I don't know.

D: What will happen next?

C: I think – I think, I will surely get another body.

D: When will that happen?

C: Yes, hm – for human beings it does seem a long time – but for us it is not so.

D: who are you? (plural)

C: Yes, we are, we are – what are we, yes, I don't know what we are – we have thoughts – I believe, we are only thoughts – we are – without body, but exactly how, I cannot tell you.

D: Is it beautiful here? This state of being?

C: Yeees, yes, but beautiful, beautiful – you know, that which one calls life and what happens – that is – how shall I say it – it is harmonious and even and quiet, however there are no heights and no depths – you know, you would call it boring, I believe –…

C: Believes she will have to get out again but tells of others who have accepted this state and are happy with it and might remain there for hundreds of years. Both C and D try to understand the present condition of ego and energy and D continues:

D: Well, then you want to return to earth?

C: Yes, alas, but I don't want a body which has to suffer such a lot -

D: Can you choose?

C: No, that I cannot do.

D: How will be the course of your new life?

C: It will be short, very short.

D: Why short?

C: Yes, I will have to suffer again – just what I didn't want, but not the soul – only the body – but the soul – she will, I believe, be rather calm, balanced, or I, – you know – that which I am now – when it is again inside the body – the body suffers – but that which I am, does not suffer – that remains quiet and…

D: Is that a progress?

C: Yes, very much.

And now D moves her on to the gradual incarnation – the alignment with matter. She had also to explain the cause of the paralysis in her left arm – the consequence of a kick by a horse in the Baron's stable during an amorous approach by her, then pregnant mother to be, to the Baron. At the Baron's rebuff the horse was startled. During the last phase of the session D helps C to come to terms and to see the historical aspect of her encounter with rats and with the paralised arm. Her death occurred on 13th January 1826. She is now able to view the whole sequence of events and Detlevsen concludes: "We shall now soon conclude this session. You will be quite awake and in your waking-state all the information from this session will be fully at your disposal. In any case you will feel very, very well.

This much abbridged version was included in order to give the reader a taste of the sincere and responsible way Thorwald Dethlevsen is pursuing his past-life therapy. Earlier in the text he makes the following observation:

Originally soul-care and medical art were invested in one hand, namely that of the priest. With 'priest' I don't mean what is understood in our time, but those wise men who knew about the laws of nature and of the cosmos and from this knowledge had the ability to help and to heal. The dividing of this profession in churchly pastors, psychotherapists and physicians did not amount to the greater welfare of man. A renewed unification of these three branches of knowledge would be of benefit for the suffering human being. Psychotherapy has today the chance to further such a development.

Roger Woolger's book 'Other Lives, Other Selves' offers an important addition to the list of such testimonies...

Dr. Roger J. Woolger PhD
discovers reincarnation (USA)

'Other Lives, Other Selves – A Jungian Psychotherapist Discovers Past Lives' is a remarkable work by a master in his field. Trained in the Jungian discipline, building on the vast collective unconscious of mankind as well as the personal unconscious, he was initially a strong sceptic regarding reincarnation. Known for this, he was invited to review 'Cathars and Reincarnation' (published in the 1970's) by Dr Arthur Guirdham. As a trained psychologist, he focused on the concept of transference, arguing the patient's influence on the researcher and vice versa, giving no credit to the substance of the book. Woolger studied and settled in the US. In league with other postgraduates, and out of curiosity, they explored self-hypnosis with the question ; "Was there a past life"? To their great surprise and consternation, Woolger found himself as a southern Italian, serving as a mercenary in the Papal-French crusade against the Cathars. In the chapter he called: 'A very unglamorous Past Life' he saw himself involved in the brutal slaughter of heretics. Later, disgusted by the whole crusade, he switched sides, only to be caught and burned on the stake. This rather shattering story was the first encounter with his own past life and the reality of reincarnation.

The method Woolger applied in his clinical work was not reliant, as was Dethlefsen, on a hypnotically induced state of trance. He asked his clients to lie down and shut their eyes. He then let them repeat phrases they had uttered several times before, such as 'I am too young for it', 'It is all too much for me', etc.

As the therapist, he would take the lead with questions that probed right into the underlying problem. He was convinced that he had to regress the client to the painful core and agony of a past incident. The client was also always consciously engaged with the evaluation that followed. This often became a turning point in their lives. Dethlefsen, to the contrary, was left with the choice either to cause his 'subjects' to remember, or to forget, what had been revealed during the session. Woolger's book is rich with past life stories which are suitably used as examples for searching commentaries.

Part I of his book briefly charts his own personal and professional evolution from a Jungian analyst to a Jungian past life therapist. Part II describes how he has developed a synthesis of various ideas and techniques currently favoured by certain transpersonal psychotherapists. Part III looks at two specific factors he finds essential in past life work which come to expression in body and soul. Part IV describes the momentous and pivotal experiences of birth and death, as they occur in past life work. The final chapter tries to put the work in the broader perspective of spiritual development and Jung's concept of individuation. Woolger knows that he could have presented much of the material in simpler ways and used fewer technical terms, but the picture is a complex one and he has attempted to do it justice. He finishes the Preface by saying: "Like early maps of the New World, this is only a sketch of new and unfamiliar territory. In charting these unknown coasts, there are more than a few inspired guesses, with the result that some parts may be hopelessly out of proportion, or just plain wrong. I hope future explorers will correct my misperceptions and unwitting distortions."

In view of the remarkable volume of research and pioneering thoughts, one cannot but applaud the author for what he has achieved and shared with his readers in such humble, yet convincing terms and thereby adding his voice unequivocally in confirmation and acceptance of reincarnation and karma as a truth and fact of life. Woolger, however insists that he did not set out to prove this fact; it was, and is, his task as a psychotherapist to help and, if possible, heal people suffering from otherwise unexplained and incurable complexes of phobias, guilt, withdrawals, anger and a sense of abandonment.

As a student of Rudolf Steiner, I was naturally astonished to read that Roger Woolger had the following to say: "Rudolf Steiner's higher spiritual leagues do not appeal to me." He continued: "I prefer to remain dumb before the vast and miraculous interweaving and re-absorption of soul and the myriad of heights and depths of the psyche, seeking to know itself." An opportunity missed. Steiner could have shed light on various questions Woolger is skirting, such as regarding the true nature of the core of the human being, the difference between soul and spirit, its past and future and the nature of the interim period between lives on earth. It is one of the signs of our time that the work of Steiner has continually received, in spite of his very public work, a similar response as that given by Woolger.

He sees himself as a 'discoverer' and pioneer of the truth of reincarnation and noticed that many of his fellow psychologists have lost the meaning of psyche, the human soul, and detected in them a certain 'psycho phobia. Could the same apply to

Woolger himself in regard to the spirit? The Eastern concepts lack the essential individual aspect on which Steiner's Western spirituality, or esotericism is built. Does Woolger suffer from, what could be called 'pneuma phobia', an aversion to considering the reality of the spirit ? The chapter on karma and reincarnation from Steiner's book 'Theosophy' is presented in a condensed form in chapter six of this book, where the concept of 'spirit' and the difference to 'soul' is clearly pointed out.

How Karma works

(quoted from 'Other Lives, Other Selves' by Rodger J Woolger). The following text is of special interest from the point of synchronicity with Arthur Guirdham.

"But back in the 1970s, knowing nothing of this, Jung's considered position that reincarnation was in principle unprovable but was nevertheless one of the most widespread of all religious beliefs and must in itself be accorded the status of an archetype, a universal psychic structure. – This was still how I thought in 1971, when I was sent a book called The Cathars and Reincarnation to review for the prestigious Journal of the Society for Psychical Research in London. I had been a member of this long established society – the first ever to scientifically investigate mediumship, telepathy, apparitions, etc.- since college days and Renee Haynes, the Journal's editor, knew that I tempered my interest in such matters with a healthy skepticism. – As it happened, The Cathars and Reincarnation, by Arthur Guirdham, proved to be an event which Jungians call 'synchronistic' because it anticipated a path I was later to take. ... By way of explanation of the title of this unusual book, I should say that the Cathars, also called the Albigensians were a heretical medieval sect that flourished in Italy and the southern France in the thirteenth century. The Cathar heresy became so widespread that eventually the Church had to (my emphasis) mount a full-scale crusade to exterminate it. It was during this crusade, incidentally, in which upward of a half million people were burned or otherwise massacred, that the so-called Holy Inquisition was set up." ...

"To the psychoanalyst in training it all sounded like what we call in the trade 'Transference' and 'countertransference'. Transference is the patient's unconscious emotional involvement with the thera-pist, and countertransference is the therapist's recipro-cal feelings, if they exist. In a good analysis, the thera-pist's job is to spot when this is happening in both himself and the client. ... This is pretty much what I said in the review of Guirdham's book, and Renee Haynes agreed with my conclusions. Guirdham went on to write several more books about other reincar-nated Cathar friends, and the whole thing began to sound like a reincarnational soap opera."

"A Very Unglamorous Past Life"

"This was in the early 1970s. More and more absorbed in the psychology of Jung, I forgot all about Guirdham, Catharism, and reincarnation. By 1976 I had settled in America, Vermont to be precise. ... The next time the subject of past lives came up was when a college friend of mine suggested experimenting with a technique for regressing oneself to a past life. I was skeptical, but agreed to the experi-ment. Jungian training had taught me much about working with visualization and dream imagery in a relaxed, meditative state. So why not? – Imagine my surprise, now eight years after that review, lying on a sofa in a remote farmhouse in Vermont, when images, at first dimly, then very vividly began to form, and I not only found myself in southern France, but in the thick of the Albigensian crusade! Here I was, now a practising Jungian analyst, having visions that my own training had told me were impossible. Had the visions resembled the stories in Guirdham's book, my skepticism would immediately have been alerted. But my story, as it unfolded, was not at all focused on the persecuted minor lords and ladies of Languedoc. Quite in reverse. I found myself almost grunting out the story of a very crude peasant-turned-mercenary soldier of that same period. This rough-and-ready character I seemed to have assumed was originally from the south of Naples and ended up in the papal army raised by the King of France to exterminate the heresy in the South. As this highly unsavory individual, I found myself in the thick of some of the most hideous massacres, in which the inhabitants of whole French cities were hacked to pieces and burned in huge pyres in the name of the Church. – Images from that first remembrance haunted me for years, and it took three more two-hour regressions to complete the story I was, and still am, loathe to look at. Yet, amazingly, it started to explain to me disturbing fragments of torture and killing that had come in dreams, meditation, and unbidden fantasy over the years, images that no amount of psychotherapy had ever really touched. Also, the way the story ended seemed to explain a phobia, a fear of fire, I have had all my life. After one of the sieges, the mercenary I seem to have been, deserted and joined the heretics, eventually only to be caught and burned at the stake himself. – As I reflected on the story more and more, other pieces of my personal history in this life started to fall into place. Since adolescence I had developed a very cynical attitude to almost all orthodox religion, especially Christianity. I found it hard to see any Church as anything but authoritarian and dogmatic, denying people the freedom of personal inquiry and experiment. But even more adamant had been my early rejection of all forms of militarism and a strong inclination toward pacifism. I even refused to join the Boy Scouts for reasons I could scarcely articulate as a teenager. Could it be that from early on I had unconsciously been reminded of parts of that soldier's brutal experience?"

Dr Joel L. Whitton and Joe Fisher
– discovers life between lives

Joel L Whitton, PhD, is a Toronto-based psychiatrist whose work was presented in 'Life Between Life' co-authored by himself and the writer Joe Fisher. The Introduction to this says of Whitton:

"A strong believer in reincarnation he uses hypnosis to take his patients back into their former lives in order to uncover the origins of traumas and neuroses afflicting them."

Fisher started his writing career as a reporter in England. Since then he has worked for newspapers on both sides of the Atlantic. He now lives in Toronto.

He is the author of the international bestseller 'The Case for Reincarnation'(published by Grafton Books).

Whitton met a surprise during one of his regression sessions, when, having been slightly inaccurate with his instruction to one of his subjects in trance, instead of details emerging of a former life, a scene was described which pointed to an existence between two incarnations. He 'discovered' empirically the 'Bardo', (a Tibetan expression for the interim period between incarnations). This period is of great importance for the retrospective evaluation of the previous life experiences and also for a looking forward to a new life, with a renewed purpose of correcting past mistakes. Although a reference was made to the three judges or guides, the emphasis was on the functional and beneficial side of the assessment, and not trying to gain a deeper insight in this realm of existence.

Fisher made Whitton's acquaintance in Toronto, where both of them had their home. Whitton had acquired fame as a psychiatrist for his successes in past-life therapies. Yet, his own conviction concerning reincarnation is not shared by the majority of fellow psychiatrists and psychologists.

Fisher was about to publish a book 'The Case for Reincarnation' and wanted to include Whitton's work of past-life therapies as one of the chapters. When he approached Whitton, he was told that the doctor had no interest in publicity. To his surprise, two years later, Whitton's secretary phoned and invited Fisher for a discussion with Whitton regarding his new project. This was in October 1984. The new project was a 'chance discovery of the intermission between incarnations'.

This meeting between the two men then lead to a fruitful collaboration. Fisher was given access to Whitton's research records. In Fisher's words, he was given 'the keys to the castle keep'.

Joe Fisher thus presented Dr Whitton's work in 'Life Between Life, Scientific Explorations into the Void Separating One Life from the Next'. The book consists of four sections: 1) The general and philosophical part; 2) Seven Karmic Case Studies; 3) The Meaning of the Interim and, 4) on Self-Exploration.

This lucidly written work tries to shed light on the positive influences in the sequence of reincarnations that stem from this interim region. It describes the totally different 'nature' of the state of being in this realm as 'unspeakable', as 'unimaginable'. Fisher has placed as the motto over this chapter, words by Rudolf Steiner: "Life between death and a new birth is as rich and varied as life here between birth and death…". Essential for Whitton is the fact that he himself 'stumbled' on this discovery. In 1973 he had embarked to determine by experiment and controlled study the legitimacy of hypnotic regression as a means of investigating reincarnation. This project was conducted in conjunction with the medical committee of the Toronto Society for Psychical Research. By then the popularity of regressive hypnosis had far outstripped scientific knowledge of the subject. Many publications had already appeared and it was timely to present a scientifically approved study.

The project was publicised and volunteers invited for hypnotic experiments. From 50 applicants, Whitton chose a woman of stable character, regular employment, unexceptional lifestyle and behaviour and deeply hypnotizable. Four of her former, all female, incarnations had been explored, the last two in North America, one in Portugal during the 13th century and one at the time of Genghis Khan.

During trance, Dr Whitton interrupted his subject when she described details from her 19th century life and said: "Go to the life before you were Martha", expecting to home in on the previous incarnation, when for several minutes no words came from her lips. Instead she was rapidly flicking her eyelids and her lips moved; she seemed to be searching for words, when slowly and with great difficulty she announced in a dreamy monotone: "I'm in the sky... I can see a farmhouse and a barn... it is early, early morning. The sun is low... and making shadows across burnt fields... stubble fields." Whitton was puzzled: He did not say: "go to the incarnation before you were Martha," but had said "go to the life before...". By putting further questions he became convinced that "... by accident" he had "... stumbled" upon the "... Bardo". From that time on he gave particular attention to this state of being and the significance it has for each following incarnation.

Fisher sums up and explains the concept of this interim, void, 'space between' and the significance it had in many cultures throughout the ages; from the Egyptian and Tibetan 'Book of the Dead', the Bardo, right to the Middle Ages and the purgatory. He refers to the images of the scale for the weighing of the soul, discusses the different figures that officiate as judges. He notes that a great change of attitude has taken place over the ages. Karma as retribution and punishment has changed to making compensation and even as presenting the opportunity for improving the whole karmic situation. The three judges often described, have now taken on more the attitude of counsellors.

In the chapter 'The Cosmic Classroom' we read 'Karma is that which individuals have set in motion for themselves from lifetime to lifetime by their motivations, attitude and behaviour.

As mentioned, Fisher observes the great changes that have taken place in the perception of karma from the punishment and retribution aspect to the compensatory one. All the ancient cultures, whether Hebrew or Icelandic, had the 'eye for eye and tooth for tooth' principle, a never-ending chain of revenge. Even today this attitude unfortunately still survives, but is experienced as an anachronism. Fisher traces a thread back to Christian Gnostics and Hebrew Kabalists who fostered and promoted the aspect of compensation. He goes on to show how karma is now considered as being a cosmic classroom, the origin of this understanding Fisher places vaguely in the European Middle Ages.

This requires the following correction: It was Gotthold Ephraim Lessing, (1729-1781), who, as a brilliant scholar, writer and philosopher, wrote the treatise 'The Education of the Human Race', in which he compared the whole historical process as one of learning. In the early stages it was necessary to enforce with the power of outer authority what the Ten Commandments and other laws demanded. With the increase of maturity the outer observation of the Law was ever more interiorised, until man, through his own insight, could become the originator of an individualised moral code, in freedom. (We may remember here the words, "For the Law was given by Moses, but grace and truth came by Jesus Christ". John 1-17)

Lessings far-reaching thoughts reveal a man of genius, who was forced to publish his treatise under a pseudonym for the protection of his reputation. It was at the same time a public confession to his conviction of reincarnation.

In spite of Fisher's own brilliant thoughts and, on the whole, a truthful presentation of ideas derived from the occupation with the theme of reincarnation and karma, a generalisation and shortcut to the truth is evident. It is necessary to recognise Beings behind processes! In this matter, natural science needs the extension of spiritual science.

Dr Helen Wambach PhD –
probes into life before birth

Helen Wambach, PhD – Probes into Life before Birth. From her book 'Life before Life'

Helen Wambach is an exceptional psychologist. She was teaching her subject for many years and found it increasingly boring to teach. So she chose a different task and turned to research. She was aware of Dr Raymond Moody's book 'Life after Life'. She had become aware of the ever more urgent question involving human consciousness, and of what is remembered from the intra-uterine period before birth. Her situation is expressed in the following words: "This hunger for a deeper understanding is very widespread in our culture. Some are trying to return to the certitudes of the old tribal religions, accepting unquestioningly doctrines laid down thousands of years ago. Their hope is that by returning to an earlier innocence and an earlier dependence on the mysteries of an unknowable god, we can save ourselves from the consequences of our own acts. Others have seen that there is no return. We did become reasoning creatures who used our brain to understand the physical universe. We did become gods in terms of the miracles we could bring about on earth. But now we must become gods in our profounder understanding of who we are, where we come from, and what our purpose must be".

She undertook with her research something she called 'a kind of Gallop-poll' (so-called because the Gallup Organisation is well known for providing statistical services). She conducted group workshops of volunteers willing to be hypnotized and given research questions to be answered after returning to day-waking consciousness. In Chicago she had 54 volunteers encamped on the floor of a hall. Sitting on a chair she started to speak with a gentle voice making her subjects feel relaxed and soon responding to her suggestions, they went into a trance.

The text on the back cover of her book tells of "... the extraordinary book that explores the fascinating answers and questions asked of 750 subjects under hypnosis about life before birth. Dr Wambach's two-year study persuaded her that '90% of the people who come to me had definitely a flash of images from a past life... I am convinced that the time has come to study rigorously the plausibility of reincarnation'."

The questions and their answers with commentary make up the chapters of the book. They are: 'Did you choose to be born? Why did you choose the 20th century? Have you chosen your sex for this coming life? Have you known your mother to-be in a past life? Are you aware now, before you are born, of others you will know in the coming lifetime? Will you know them as lovers or mates? Will you know them as friends? Will they be your children?'

Whilst Wambach placed her research firmly on the assumption of the truth of reincarnation, supported by the answers she received, She still feels answerable to the present paradigm of science with her references to the right part of the brain being in tune with the subconscious, and applying the knowledge of brain-wave cycles per second and biofeedbacks to her subjects in seeking to understand these phenomena

Before she worked with her Chicago group, on which the book is based, she had conducted, at least 400 times, the 'birth trip' with various other subjects. Altogether she has records of 2000 subjects. In her description 'How I did the Research' she states: "The words ran in my mind like a loop of tape, and I learned how my thoughts could stray from what my voice was saying, and I heard my voice come from a distance. I knew I was in an altered state of consciousness while I was conducting these sessions." This experience allowed her to accompany her instructions with self-reflections.

She spoke in a soothing tone of voice that allowed her subjects to relax and their everyday-consciousness drift away. From a corner of the room she felt some resistance. Fully accepting the reality of telepathy she directed her reassuring thoughts in that direction and there was acceptance. Proceeding with her instructions, she said: 'now your body is lying heavy on the floor, deeply relaxed. Your body is so heavy it feels as though it's sinking very gently into the floor. But your mind is free and light, floating, alert, yet deeply comfortable and relaxed. I want you to imagine, now, that you are a pinpoint of consciousness floating up away from your body and hovering near the ceiling of this room. You can perceive a dim light, and you are looking down now from a vantage point near the ceiling of this room. Can you see my body sitting in the chair here? My legs are crossed; my arms are resting on the arms of the chair. Now look and see if you can find your body on the floor. Can you see the others around you?'

With this quote you can see the relationship Wambach is building up as a preparation for her actual quest. She has established that out-of-body consciousness, this consciousness of self, free from the body, on which she now focuses with her instructions into the prenatal and the birth experience. Speaking further on the past and the future where always choices had been, or are to be made, she defines free will in the following way: 'You may choose to remember parts of your past life, since forgotten, and you may choose to realize their potential in the future that is also yours to choose. This is what is meant by free will'.

These fragments describing her method of conducting her workshops may suffice.

When Wambach returned her subjects to ordinary consciousness she found them relaxed and happy. But of the returned questionnaires only around half had given answers and only 40% were consistent and describing genuine observations, unhampered by the interfering intellect. Nonetheless there was a broad consensus of answers to her questions, which she has evaluated statistically.

The main volume of the book consists of the individual answers to the specific questions with commentaries by Helen Wambach. They are very interesting in themselves in all their personal differences. But here only a summary remark may be justified based on the general consensus found to the following issues: There is consciousness before birth, even before conception; there are Beings who help the incarnating soul making the decision with their wisdom and determination; there are many choices to be made before taking that step according to individual karma – some are less free than others. Even the choice of gender, determined by considerations whether it serves the overall aim in life better to be incarnated in a female or male body. Other questions were answered by some and not by others.

Whatever view one might have regarding the probing into the realm of the unborn, many important questions are called up which are ever more essential to consider. One reflective passage by Wambach will illustrate this, preceded by quoting the experience of one of her subjects:

"I see now that I was thinking of myself in a much too narrow and restricted sense. I feel in touch now with my dreaming self, as well as with my waking self. I don't take the happenings of every day with such seriousness as I did before. It's as though I have a different perspective now each day of my life, and more of an inner serenity in dealing with the ups and downs that are inevitable".

"While it is very gratifying to hear these experiences of my subjects, I feel that the broadening of self-awareness that they have experienced after the workshop is part of their own development and not due to anything I might have said or done. I have the strong feeling that people were drawn to my workshop because they were at a certain point of their lives where they were ready and open to new experiences. They used my hypnotic inductions, my questions, my suggestions, as a way to open up. Some other experiences could have served just as well to bring them to this self-awareness; I don't feel it's a magic within my hypnotic workshops. It's a magic within my subjects, ready to unfold."

This unpretentious attitude pervades all her pioneer work. Wambach's humanity finds an especially imaginative expression in the last chapter: 'Finding Truth on the All-American Talk Show'. She describes vividly the characters of those who had been invited by the host to guarantee a heated discussion. She shows their special bent and one-sided prejudice against her. Then she describes the event where it was difficult to speak a coherent sentence before being interrupted. After the end of the Talk Show everyone left in the same frame of mind with which they had arrived.

Then she followed this with an imaginative dream of after images: She ascended on high and met a figure surrounded by a white light, emanating love and wisdom and confirming her in her search for truth. Then did arrive her opponents one after another. The lady from the Christian Family Foundation saw in the figure she met, the Christ. He explained everything to her and she left happily. Then came the gentleman from the Committee to investigate the Paranormal; after his conversation he was convinced that he had talked with Einstein who had explained to him the Theory of Relativity. The next was convinced that he had the pleasure of making Freud's acquaintance; and again another who met his grandfather, who once was an inspiration to him. Everyone was confirmed in his or her own mindset and yet helped to a tolerant attitude by accepting also other people's point of view.

Chapter 2

Witnesses of Reincarnation and Karma

Joan Grant – remembering many lifetimes

With much respect and gratitude do I look back to my own meeting with Joan Grant and Denys Kelsey in 1979 and the hospitality they had shown to me. Her many fascinating books based on her far-memory have been a source of stimulation for my many questions.

—⁓—

Joan was born on 12 April 1907 into a well-to-do, upper middle-class family in England, Jack and Blanche Marshall, before the First World War. During her first seven years she still experienced the glory of the British Empire. Her father was a scientist who received the CBE for his work on British mosquitoes, for which he had built a laboratory at his own home. He was also a tennis champion.

Her mother was a queenly matron with decisive demeanour and extraordinary gifts. She had foreseen the sinking of the Titanic in 1912, and also the imminent collapse of the roof of an indoor tennis court, thereby saving the lives of the workmen.

Joan tells that she was conceived in the Blue Grotto on Capri. Her favourite person was her

Grandmother, Jenny, who died when Joan was 18 months old, and yet accompanied her through life. Of her early childhood Joan relates the following:

"The resentment I felt in finding myself trapped in the body of a baby flared up soon afterwards. Perhaps the long flat beach (on Hayling Island), the sand dunes with their harsh, bleached grasses, the restless sound of the sea stirred latent memories in me. I was not always Joan, but sometimes a Greek boy, training to be a runner on a hotter, brighter shore".

Such feelings in a little child, though verbalised much later, accompanied Joan throughout her life.

At 4 ½ years, whilst playing, a propped-up heavy door fell on the child severely bruising her body and breaking a leg.

Joan grew up watched over by nannies, governesses and servants. Many visitors called on her parents. Her many detailed memories are retold in a lively style.

In 1914 she went with her family on a visit to the USA and miraculously returned safely home after the declaration of war. After her return she entered a girls' boarding school, which she disliked. At assembly the headmistress told the girls that a bird had whispered to her that many of them had not confessed to their sins, which should have been declared in writing. Quaking with anger Joan got up and shouted at her: 'you are a wicked old woman! God never sent His dove to sneak to you – for such a black lie He should strike you dead!' This kind of spontaneous and decisive trait was a hallmark of Joan's character, the consequences of which caused her much suffering.

It was, however, not only her own suffering she was destined to bear. During the later war years "I used to find myself on a battlefield, grown-up and usually in the uniform of a Red Cross nurse, although occasionally I was a stretcher-bearer. I knew I had reported for duty and received specific orders; either to explain to a man who had just been killed that he was safely dead, or to encourage him to return to a body that was not due to die yet although it had been severely wounded."

When telling others, including her parents, about it, it only attracted reprimand and ridicule. Yet once she found one of the recuperating officers, stationed at her house, alone at breakfast; and joining him, told him: 'Last night I was with a man called McAndrew, when he was killed. I can describe the regimental badge, although I cannot remember the name of the regiment, except that it was not an English one. And I can tell you the slang name of his trench'. The man was able to identify the regiment by the description. It was Canadian. Soon afterwards he wrote to Joan's Father: 'for heaven's sake, don't laugh at the child. I cannot attempt an explanation, but I have checked what she said … A private called McAndrew was among the killed. She was even correct about the local name of the front-line trench.'

Two other episodes attest to her intelligence and determination:

Prompted by her father's scientific research, in which she was assisting him, and the encouragement by a teacher, she wanted to prepare herself for entry to Cambridge for the study of the sciences. Her mother had employed a tutor to assist Joan in her studies, but took a dislike to her and insisted on dismissing her; whereupon, Joan gave her parents an ultimatum: if this lady tutor (with whom she had struck up a friendship) is dismissed, she will not take up her study at Cambridge. Joan was only 15 at the time and, as her Mother did not change her mind, Joan gave up all formal education.

The second striking event was the following: Joan danced all alone by full moon on the tennis court; she did it so forcefully that she snapped a tendon. As a result she had to spend weeks and months on sofas and in wheelchairs, a severe trial to her patience. It was made clear to her that she would never play her favourite tennis again. Her Mother suggested that she should play golf instead. Overcoming her dislike for this sport, she asked for and studied golf literature. Without ever having played at golf, she secretly enlisted herself for the next tournament. Having studied physical science, together with her strong determination, she managed the unimaginable. Only days after her leg was out of plaster, and just able to stand, she was taken to the championship. The extra-ordinary result was blazing the next morning from the front page of the Daily Chronicle: 'Girl Golf Wonder! Sixteen year-old player carries off five awards in Hants County Championship!' The proud father carried the cutting always in his wallet he was taken in her dreams to the battlefields and trenches and had to suffer the horrors of combat with the soldiers. Of these frequent and exhausting events she writes:

—∿—

On one occasion during the absence of her parents she played host to a family friend, the writer and historian H G Wells. When listening to some of her night-duty stories he was much impressed and encouraged her to become a writer, once she had gathered more life-experience.

When still a teenager she was wooed, but shortly before the wedding she decided not to go through with it: she would only be a burden to him. Within days she made arrangements to go skiing in Switzerland. Her Mother assumed that her lady friend was accompanying Joan as a chaperone, but the friend was already at the resort. Without sufficient cash Joan went on her journey third class but did not like the company and placed herself in a first class compartment. When the 'chef du train' came along, expecting her to pay the excess, she invited him to sit down and sang to him. She managed to cast her spell and so he invited her to occupy a sleeper compartment – gratis.

On arrival at the hotel she met an old acquaintance, and fell in love, which led to a surprise engagement. Yet her fiancée soon lost his life in an accident. She returned to London and met again, by surprise, the man who became her understanding and supportive husband – Denis Grant. A daughter, Gillian, joined them soon afterwards. So much of the early life of a determined and exceptional woman.

Denis Grant became an archaeologist and Joan followed him to Iraq for two seasons of excavating, and her clairvoyant faculties helped often to find a more truthful answer. In 1935 they spent three weeks in Egypt, which stirred some inner responses in Joan. Only later, back in England, and when visiting an elderly relation did the gates to her far memory start to open up. The lady, Daisy, possessed five scarabs and Joan was asked to try psychometry, i.e. placing an object to her forehead which can result in tuning into the vibrations for which the object is a catalyst. Of the five, only the last one was genuine ancient Egyptian. This experiment resulted in Joan recalling extraordinary and detailed images and happenings from her own past in Egypt as a temple priestess in training for remembering past lives. Her name then was Sekeeta. In the 115 recollections which followed, her husband wrote them down as he listened (some 120, 000 words) and this was then condensed into her first book 'Winged Pharaoh' (1937).

The recollections were occasionally spontaneous, but more often arranged for the evening, often with guests present. She changed her level of consciousness and then described in words what she experienced. At the same time she was dependent on speedwriting or shorthand, before electronic recordings were invented.

In order to allow Joan a smooth return from her often very trying experiences of the recalled past, it was agreed that soft music should sound at the end of a session. At such an occasion a musician was present who expressed interest to know what sort of music was produced in ancient Egypt. Joan then changed her level of consciousness again but the string instrument she met was the guitar – not an Egyptian instrument – and this led to her discovery of life as Carola in 16th century Italy. Many other former lives took on shape during her changed consciousness. Of all this Joan gives accounts in her books 'Far Memory' and 'Many Lifetimes'. The latter was written jointly with Denys Kelsey.

Life did not become easier, both for herself and others, by identifying consciously with so much detailed knowledge of the past. It was difficult for her husband to realise that this private knowledge was suddenly shared with others and was also about to be published.

An occasion had arisen in London, when Joan showed her typed copy of 'Winged Pharaoh' to an old family friend. He, a very sceptical literary professional, listened to her story with great reservations, but begged, however, to read her copy. Much impressed, he insisted that this should definitely be published. He had a friend who was a printer and so the way from private to public went with astonishing ease, but also with personal consequences.

During the war she found herself running a large household and catering for many evacuees in Cornwall where she practised many hands-on practical skills. Also later on in Scotland she cared for some people with special medical and psychiatric needs and showed extraordinary talent to cope with unusual demands.

After a visit by Denys Kelsey, a meeting that lasted into the small hours of the night, a mutual recognition came about which led to a fruitful partnership in her later life. The jointly-written 'Many Lifetimes' conveys a good impression of their working together.

By himself, Kelsey had come to a kind of stasis in his psychiatric practice. Certain diagnoses, based on the one-life theory, did not lead to satisfactory insights. Kelsey had heard of Joan Grant and her far-memory and knowledge of former lives. What he found in meeting her was both an extension of his knowledge, as well as an existential answer.

In the above-mentioned book is a chapter called 'An Assortment of Apparitions'. Here Joan reveals another side of herself: clairvoyance and a readiness to help parts of entities, which were separated from their proper identity, to unite again. This is no exorcising of ghosts, but healing with insight. She offers many important explanations on the different parts of the human being. She gives a particularly good description of the Supra-Physical Body, known in spiritual science as life-body or ether-body. She sees it as an energy-field, building up and maintaining the physical particles. Based on her familiarity with reincarnation she also makes a clear distinction between personality and individuality or, in her terminology, the Integral Personality. Her close collaboration with Denys Kelsey led them both to an enhanced understanding of human nature, of illness and health, and a higher degree of effectiveness in their healing efforts.

The index-like references to Joan Grant's life and work can hardly do justice to the lively presentation of so many fascinating events and encounters that have taken place in this, her latest life.

From what she has written in a dozen books a progression toward humility and service to others is evident. Instructive, too, is the realisation that she and Kelsey were close to each other in Roman times, where he, too, was a physician. In the present life, love has shown itself as a powerful agent for transformation and development, enhancing the striving for the good and for healing.

—⁂—

The following text is given as an example of one of Joan Grant's regressions induced by a genuine scarab, held to her forehead while reclining on a couch. Leslie, her husband was writing down Joan's description of her experience.

"The moment it touched my forehead I knew it was warm and lively. 'This one is much older than any of the others. It was taken from a mummy of a priestess... . Leslie, do you remember the underground tomb we went to at Sakkara, the one with three drop-stones in the entrance passage to the inner chamber, shaped like Noah's ark? It wasn't a tomb. It was a place where rememberers, priests of Anubis, were taken for their initiation. The place I am seeing is not the one we went to but is very like it'. – I broke off for a moment as I was shivering with cold though the room was warm, so Elfie covered me with a rug. – 'This did not come off a mummy. I thought she was a mummy because she is dressed as though ready for burial for this symbolises that her spirit is as free to travel in search of wisdom as though her earth-body had released it...' For over an hour I described what I was seeing; how a girl, called Sekeeta was taken from the temple of Atet to undergo the ordeal of initiation, during which she must leave her body for four days and four nights, returning at the end of the fourth day to dictate to a scribe what she had experienced. Then the degree of identification deepened. 'Though I am alive, I must be as the dead; no longer can my body be unto me a friendly refuge to which I can fly when the powers of darkness are too strong; nor can I return to my body to protect it when the evil ones would turn it into a prison of pain. How shall I be as a beacon of light among the people when my heart is beating as though it would leap from the cage of my ribs? Shall I ever see the sun again? Will my body ever obey my will gently and pleasantly again? Shall I be as Hekhet who failed, yet did not die, and sits in the courtyard with blind eyes and wet sagging lips, trapped in a body that only flies dare to touch? Soon, soon, they will put the mask upon my face. My eyelids must not flutter. If my body is not beneath my will, how can any of them who see me believe my speech, even though it be the mirror of the gods? I can feel the boat tilting. It has left the water. They are lowering it down the shaft. It is very cold in the passage. I can feel the darkness through my closed eyelids. I can feel the mask upon my face. Soon I shall hear the drop-stones fall. It is as though I were living in a great gong. The falling stones shatter the stillness, but soon it will return. I must quiet the beating of my heart: it sounds in my ears loudly so that I cannot hear the voice of my wisdom. Be still, my body, be still and not unworthy; for I would make you an instrument worthy to receive that which I shall be told. I must remember clearly, clearly … .' – A long way away a voice was calling my name. No, not my name, someone else's name. 'Joan – come back, Joan'. A quiet voice, but insistent. Reluctantly I opened my eyes. Leslie was leaning over me, briskly rubbing my hand, from which he had removed the scarab. 'Come back now. You have been out quite long enough.' – Memory started to slide away from me like bright water flowing into a tunnel. 'Did I talk clearly enough for you to hear? Did you write it down? It was very important what I was doing – important to me. But I can't remember. – 'You need not try to remember. I have got it all written down, although part of the time you were going very fast.' The blue scarab was lying on

the table. 'There is more, so much more in it,' I said,
still not quite awake. 'Please can I do some more of it
after dinner?' – 'You have done quite enough today,'
said Leslie firmly. He looked at his watch. 'You have
never been out so long as you have today.' – Today was
the 13th of September 1936.

Edgar Cayce – the clairvoyant seer and healer

Edgar Cayce (1877-1945) is one of the most
important witnesses of repeated lives on earth. He
started his last life in rural Kentucky, USA, but moved,
already in his adolescence, to the city where he worked
as a clerk in a bookstore; later he became an insur-
ance agent. Then something happened to him, which
was to change his life: he almost lost his voice and by
necessity apprenticed himself to a photographer.

During this period of his life a hypnotist dis-
played his skills in a public gathering. When leaving,
a student of suggestive therapeutics, a Mr Lane,
approached Cayce, knowing of his predicament and
asked whether he could apply his budding hypnotic
skills on him with the object of finding out what was
wrong with his throat. Cayce agreed. Lane's idea was
to suggest that Cayce, under hypnosis, describe the
nature of his ailment. Having changed consciousness,
Cayce described, speaking in a normal voice, the condition of his own vocal chords. He started: 'yes, we
can see the body … (always using the 'we'). In the
normal state, this body is unable to speak because of
a paralysis of the inferior muscles of the vocal chords,
produced by nerve strain. This is a psychological

condition producing a physical effect. It may be removed by increasing circulation to the affected parts by suggestion while in the unconscious condition.'

Lane proudly suggested to Cayce that his circulation would increase to the affected parts and that the condition would be alleviated. The effect showed a pink complexion. After some twenty minutes the sleeping man cleared his throat and said, 'It's all right now. The condition is removed. Make the suggestion that the circulation returns to normal and after that, let the body awaken.'

After this successful self-healing session, Lane suggested to Cayce to try the same method for the help of other people, and Cayce was eager to help others.

As a boy of 10 he first read the Bible from cover to cover and intended to do this once every year. He longed to be a disciple of Christ and a preacher. But now that the opportunity of healing offered itself, he was beset with fears and self-doubting. By Lane's persuasion, however, he started on a 'career' of hypnotic trance sessions. He himself would lie down on a couch and induce his own hypnosis. Then Lane would give his suggestions. One early case was that of a little girl whose mind, after an attack of influenza, would no longer develop normally and she also suffered from a convulsive condition. Not even the finest physician was able to help her and even predicted an early death.

Overcoming the doubts in his faculty, yet filled with compassion when seeing the child, he agreed to enter the hypnotic state. Guided by Lane's suggestions, Cayce stated that the girl had a fall from a carriage prior to the influenza attack, and that the germs had settled in the afflicted area, thus causing the convulsive attacks. Proper osteopathic adjustments would relieve the pressures and would return to normal. The mother confirmed the fact that the child had fallen from a carriage; it had never occurred to her, however –there being no apparent injury – that this could have any relationship to the girl's abnormal condition. The adjustments were made and the girl developed normally.

This incident and many others to follow were recorded in shorthand and transcribed with a copy retained on file. With the newspapers getting hold of this and other stories, Cayce's fame spread throughout the region and beyond. He began to receive long-distance calls and telegrams from desperate people who wanted his help. It was then that he learned it was possible to conduct 'readings' at a distance, provided he was given the exact name, the location at the time the reading was to be made, the street, town and state. Often he would begin by making some comment on the surroundings of the person, such as 'pretty rough wind here this morning' or, 'Winterthur, Switzerland: Isn't it pretty!'

Cayce prepared himself for a session by taking off his shoes, opening the top button of his shirt, lying down with his head pointing south and relaxing completely. He then put himself into trance. Lane, or Cayce's wife, later also his son, would give him the appropriate suggestions, following an agreed formula. He did not accept money, unless it was for fares or direct expenses. He rejected all commercial involvement with questions, such as: which is going to be the winning horse in a race, or being asked to appear with a turban and oriental garments in a show, or where to find a hidden treasure. Cayce refused all tempting offers. Neither did he permit any advertising. Many local people knew him only from the Sunday school. He was approached through personal contacts. With increasing demands he gave up his trade as a photographer, but remained fundamentally non businesslike. One of the readings recommended that he should move to Virginia Beach, which he then did in 1927. There all his records are being kept.

At several points in his career investigators who were suspicious and sceptical of him, as he was himself, too, often confronted Cayce. One of them observed several readings, intending to expose him as a fraud. During the next few weeks the psychiatrist was able to study all the records and left convinced by their testimonies and the simple unpretentious honesty of the man.

Other men of vision and good will also appeared at various times in Cayce's life and, recognising his humanitarian and scientific importance, gave him moral and financial assistance in the uncertainties of his strange career. Even a hospital was put into operation for two years, before it had to close down because of the recession.

Then opened the next chapter in Edgar Cayce's life: A well-to-do printer from Ohio, Lammers by name, invited Cayce and his associates for a visit at the host's expense. Being also interested in astrology, he asked Cayce for his horoscope. Compliant to the suggestion given to him, Cayce went into trance and gave information in staccato fashion, finishing the reading, to the surprise of those around him, with a five word sentence: 'He was once a monk'. This statement was electrifying; neither Cayce, nor his family and friends were conversant with the idea of reincarnation. Only Lammers recognised the full implication. A lively discussion arose, including Cayce after his return to normal consciousness. All of them living in the Christian faith, had now to reconcile the idea of reincarnation with their Christian beliefs.

From then on direct questions were asked as to former lives and a distinction had to be made between 'physical-readings', the term used for the customary ones, and 'life-readings'. Cayce himself gave in trance a new formula for these life-readings:

"You will have before you (the person's name), born (his date of birth) in (his place of birth). You will give the relation of this entity and the universe, and the universal forces, giving the conditions which are as personalities, latent and exhibited, in the present life; also the former appearances on the earth plane, giving time, place, and the name; and that in each life which built or retarded the entity's development."

Then specific questions were asked and most surprising answers came to light. Through Lammers' influence the questions were extended to encompass history, including Atlantis. It would, however, go too far in the frame of this sketch to present any of these answers. Cayce himself became ever more a source of help to people around the world, suffering in body, soul and spirit, not least with the help of insight gained through life-readings.

There is an interesting detail: The new cosmic questions involving former lives caused actual headaches to the 'sleeping' Cayce. These were, however, relieved by reversing his position, allowing his head to face north.

One of the first life-readings was directed to Cayce himself: how did he acquire his extraordinary faculties? The answer was significant: (Quote from 'Many Mansions' by Gina Cerminara)

"Life-readings on Cayce himself revealed that he had been a high priest in Egypt, many centuries ago, who was possessed of great occult powers; but self-will and sensuality proved his undoing. In a later incarnation in Persia he had been a physician. Once he had been wounded in desert warfare and left to die on the sands; alone, without food, water, or shelter, he spent three days and nights in such physical agony that he made a supreme effort to release his consciousness from his body. He was successful in this attempt. This was in part the basis for his faculty in the present for releasing his mind from the limitations of the body. All his virtues and defects of the present were frankly appraised and attributed to one or another of his many previous experiences. The present lifetime was a kind of test for his soul; he had been given the opportunity to serve mankind selflessly, and thus redeem the pride, materialism, and sensuality of his past."

—∿—

In conclusion, we recognise in Cayce a unique phenomenon, demonstrating the difference between the here-and-now personality and the hidden Individuality and are allowed to have glimpses of the self-generated karma and the spiritual help in finding the opportunity to redeem it, on the path of evolutionary self-realisation in the service of humanity.

The challenge is there for all humanity to apply the same principle. As a living companion this realisation could follow us, not as a shadow, but rather go before us as an inner light. Cayce became a true Christian healer and opened up a new understanding and perception of man and the world.

In order to appreciate what Edgar Cayce gave, it is necessary to come to terms with what is called: the Akashic records. Occultism describes this as World Memory, a recording in the world-ether. Individualities, advanced in their development, have the gift to tune in with this region and are able to conduct research and can communicate details and events of the past. A parallel Christian concept is the Book of Life.

Dr Arthur Guirdham – catalyst for reincarnated Cathars

In the Introduction to his book 'We Are One another' (1974), Dr Guirdham says the following: "Nothing in this story depends on my subjective reactions to places and people. I am not the kind of person who, on the field of Waterloo, feels inevitably that he must have been Napoleon. I am naturally of a cautious and sceptical nature and am known in my family as 'Doubting Thomas'. I am astonished that the phenomena I have encountered have been revealed to me of all people. I have occupied myself with the significance of names and messages produced in dreams, visions, in states of clairaudience and dictated by discarnate entities. Because of the unusual origin of my data I have to stress all the more carefully that I was for forty years a run-of-the-mill psychiatrist. In the NHS I was the Senior Consultant in my clinical area. I hold a scientific degree as well as being a doctor of medicine. It is all the more necessary to make these points since I claim that this, my own story, is the most remarkable of its kind I have encountered."

"A few words are necessary to explain the events to which the characters in this story so frequently return. Their memories are chiefly concentrated on the years 1242 to1244. There is a remarkably generalised preoccupation with the massacre of the Inquisitors at Avignonet. This was a gesture of defiance and self-protection launched by the representatives of the Languedoc against the tyranny and cruelty of the French Catholic invaders. The Avignonet affair stimulated the French crown to cut off the dragon's head of heresy. This was the Château of Montsegur, which had for years been the centre of instruction for Cathar sympathisers and of initiation for the priest-hood. The fortress was besieged from 1243 to 1244. It was defended by a small garrison of minor nobles and sergeants-at- arms, who fought for the inde-pendence of the Languedoc and were sympathetic to Catharism. We are especially concerned with the sergeants-at arms. The characters in this book tune-in with remarkable precision to the siege, to the evacua-tion from the castle of the Cathar treasure, probably rare books, and above all, to the last celebration of the Consolamentum before the Cathars perished at the stake after capitulation. The Consolamentum was the only sacrament recognised by the Cathars. It signified a voluntary renunciation of the flesh and of attachment to the things of this world. Six of the characters in this story attended the final celebration of this rite. The major events in this story were unfolded between late August 1968 and early summer of 1972."

Four years prior to the publication of the book quoted above, Guirdham's first book, 'The Cathars and Reincarnation', was published in 1970. Unlike the second book, which deals with a group incarnation of eight former Cathars, this first book, a kind of trailblazer, presented the extraordinary experiences of one woman, referred to as Mrs Smith. For simplicity, it is easier to concentrate on this story, which opened the way for the later revelations.

In 1962 Mrs Smith made an appointment for a consultation. She suffered from nightmares accompanied by shrieks so loud that she and her husband feared that she would wake the street. The same terrifying dreams had much the same content. First these dreams occurred about once a month, but over the years had intensified and, lately, it had come two or three times weekly. The patient was in her early thirties, good looking, open, communicative and smiling.

Upon an earlier visit to hospital an electroencephalogram was taken which proved in some way positive. When Dr Guirdham saw her, he did not follow this line of investigation but listened to her story. In her childhood she had contracted a fever and was at death's door. The parents, being Catholic, invited the priest to give her the last rites. When the priest arrived with some nuns, the child became so agitated at seeing them that the doctor had to stop the procedures then and also in future. This antipathy to her Church led later in life to her excommunication, after which she joined the Church of England. As a girl of 16/17 she spontaneously became conscious of French names, which she jotted down and of which she did not know whether they referred to people or places. Even poems came to her in old French, or Langue d'Oc, which she wrote down, without understanding their significance. Ever more material of this kind gathered up and was eventually stored in the loft by her father. She also showed psychic and clairvoyant faculties foretelling certain events. This convinced her parents that she was different from the norm. But to herself she was a great riddle: was she mad, or bad? She could not appreciate her psychic gifts.

In her dreams she often called out for Roger (in the French pronunciation). On meeting her psychiatrist for the first time she was sure in herself that he was the one she once knew as Roger. What she told him only much later was the fact that, having met him, the nightmares had stopped troubling her.

In the course of further consultations Guirdham was able to convince her that her visions, clairaudience and dreams were not hallucinations or the outcome of a deranged mind, or epilepsy.

For over a year she fluctuated in revealing her inner life to him, and regretted that she had given away her secrets. In order to continue with the consultations, she withheld from him the fact that the nightmares, which had increased so much prior to the first consultation, had completely stopped after an ordeal of 19 years! Apart from the consultations she wrote dozens of letters with information to Arthur Guirdham. He took this all very seriously and wanted to find objective confirmation of what had been revealed to him, and also to visit the area in the south of France his patient so obviously was referring to. He got in touch with leading experts on Catharism and a professor of history in France, Professor Nelli, who was an expert on the Inquisition. Gradually the pieces of the jigsaw fell into place and with the help of the records of the Inquisition a coherent story was unfolding by matching the names given by Mrs Smith to actual people and places into a time sequence. All this as stated by Guirdham in the Introduction, having taken place in the 13th century. All the characters referred to through the revelations made by Mrs Smith and the eight persons the second book is based on, were accurately identified with characters living seven hundred years ago!

These books are not written as thrillers, but as clinical case histories accompanied by the searching mind of a researcher. Nonetheless, a most interesting story is unfolding, interspersed with clear insights into the mode of life the believers upheld, and the experiences made by those people so far removed from our time. This account also confirms the reality of the spiritual world, interested in bridging the gap between the earthly world and that of the spirit. It presents the active and helpful presence of guides, even by name, involved in the transmission of verifiable names and facts.

Upon reading both books one can fully concur with Arthur Guirdham's own evaluation and claim:

that "this, my own story, is the most remarkable story of its kind I have encountered".

—⚏—

Arthur Guirdham mentions Rudolf Steiner more in passing, but at a crucial point when explaining that for the Cathars Christ did not truly incarnate in the body. For Steiner, as well as the Church, this was, however, Christ's essential deed without which the 'Mystery of Golgotha', the death on the cross and His resurrection would have no significance and meaning. Rudolf Steiner's science of the spirit clearly outlines where dualism has its justification and where it misses the essence of the Trinity, both in the divine cosmic perspective as also in Man. Anthroposophy is firmly based on a threefold understanding of Man and the world.

Arnall Broxham / Jeffrey Iverson
– More Lives than One?

Based on The Bloxham Tapes of Arnall Bloxham

In this instance two names have to be introduced, that of Arnall Bloxham and of Jeffrey Iverson. Arnall Bloxham – being the originator of the 400 tapes – recorded regressions under hypnosis on which the book is based, shall be introduced first in the words of Jeffrey Iverson, the author:

"When still a child, Arnall Bloxham became convinced that he had lived before. At the turn of the (20th) century, young Bloxham's sleep had frequently been disturbed by nightmares, dreams of past ages, people and places totally unfamiliar to him in waking hours. Later he came to believe that these dreams were scenes from a past life; that like those children more recently described by the American psychologist, Professor Ian Stevenson, he had been born with some memory of another incarnation."

Bloxham recalled, "Sometimes the dreams were very pleasant and others were very disturbing. I used to wake up howling or screaming with terror when I was a boy. It was not a nice thing, to be able to remember – but, of course, I had no control over the dreams, and I used to have to get the governess or somebody to hold my hand when I went to sleep, because I was afraid of what was going to happen next."

Much later in life, Bloxham believes he accidentally found a location he knew from his dreams, a place which had been his home in some past life – "I was taking my aunt and stepmother around the countryside, we were in the Cotswolds, when I suddenly felt "this is the very road about which I used to dream". 'It was down a steep hill, trees on either side, and the road was yellow and very dusty – and in the dreams I always felt very ill because I was travelling in a coach which was suspended by thongs, leather thongs, which made the coach sway and I'd feel very seasick. And I knew that if we went down the steep hill, turned to the right, in about half a mile or so we'd come to two towers and iron gates.

"And we did this and came to Sudeley Castle and I realized that it was where I had once lived – behind those iron gates."

On that visit the castle's gates remained locked – it was not open to the public, not even to reincarnated residents! Later, Bloxham says he went again with his wife and friend. He was able to show them around without a guide, and to lead them to an Elizabethan window, which he 'knew' was there.

Young Bloxham grew up in Pershore, Worcestershire, a small country town where market gardening and plum growing were the main occupation. While still a schoolboy at Worcester Royal Grammar School, he became interested in hypnotism, referred to in those days as 'Mesmerism', and when a school friend complained of headache, young Bloxham saw it as a chance to use his skill. He never doubted for a second that it would work and it was his first success as a hypno-therapist.

Bloxham intended to become a doctor, and carried on with his study of Mesmerism, which he thought might be a useful ability for a medical man to possess. Then, when he was eighteen, the 1914-18 war intervened and Arnall Bloxham joined the Navy and served aboard Minesweepers.

Unfortunately his ambition to become a doctor collapsed. Taken ill with typhoid fever, he was assured that because he might carry infection, he could never work in a hospital.

The frustrated doctor became a hypno-therapist and, apart from naval service in both world wars, he practised the art of healing under hypnosis for more than forty years, many of them in Christchurch, New Zealand.

Bloxham finally settled in Cardiff, in South

Wales, because, as a naval lieutenant in the Second World War, he was posted to the Welsh seaport. When the war ended, he stayed on and soon began to practise hypnotherapy again.

Bloxham and his second wife, Dulcie, made a considerable impact upon the city of Cardiff. His reputation as a hypnotherapist grew rapidly, patients were soon being referred to him by doctors and psychiatrists, he gave public lectures and appeared on television, along with a dentist and a willing patient, to demonstrate that teeth could be extracted using hypnotism as an anaesthetic.

"Gradually, there was a great change of attitude of the medical profession towards hypnosis. It was unacceptable to them at first and doctors looked at us a bit askance. Later on, doctors would send members of their own families to me for treatment but seemed reluctant to refer ordinary patients. This I found a bit hypocritical. But nowadays hypnosis is quite accepted, is used in hospitals, and doctors have even come to me to ask if I would teach them to hypnotize. Perhaps because of the way things went in the past, I have declined to pass on my secrets to them individually, although they were always welcome to attend my lectures."

Today, hypnotherapy is recognized and Bloxham was President of the British Society of Hypnotherapists, in 1972, succeeding T G Warne-Berisford, who had formed the society in 1950.

But in Cardiff, Bloxham's reputation was founded not so much on hypnotherapy as on the interest he created in reincarnation and Eastern philosophy. To be a professional hypnotist seemed strange enough to his neighbours, but once a week Bloxham opened his rambling house for about thirty friends and a sprinkling of complete strangers and held one of his 'sessions'. Dulcie Bloxham served tea and biscuits and Arnall Bloxham played tape recordings of people he had hypnotized and regressed to 'a previous existence'. Afterwards, he answered questions and spoke to his audience about reincarnation and the law of karma'...

"It needs concentration, contemplation and meditation – three things that we in the West usually don't do. ... I am actually a Christian, and of course a Christian doesn't need to believe anything particularly. One of the great things, about, say, the Church of England, is it hasn't any narrow views. You can believe anything you like. And so I believe in reincarnation."

"I also believe Christ taught reincarnation and I don't think religious Christianity today is anything like the sort of thing Christ taught. The Church of Rome started trimming it up and making it quite a different thing. You see, much of our religion is dogma – the enemy of progress and knowledge."

Bloxham will argue strongly for his belief in reincarnation and regression. But he does accept that occasionally during a regression a hypnotized person appears to make a mistake when speaking about a past time. "Some discrepancies you are bound to get, because it's only a question of memory. Even if a person is sitting a Bachelor of Arts examination, they can still get things wrong."

Even this shortened text will give some impression of this man and his way of life and work.

What is significant is that he may be considered among the pioneers of this approach to research.

Jeffrey Iverson also resident in Cardiff, is the author of the book and was a television producer with the BBC. In addition to documentaries for various BBC channels, he was an editor for a weekly TV current affairs programme in Wales. 'More Lives Than One?' – his first book, has been shown in the form of a BBC documentary. Iverson was a complete outsider to the idea of reincarnation and karma and was fundamentally sceptical to spiritual and occult aspects of life.

Bloxham had a certain fame in Cardiff and Iverson had the idea to make acquaintance with this old man. He writes:

"My first meeting with Arnall Bloxham was in October 1974. I called at his home to see if it would be worthwhile offering the BBC a television programme about this legendary old man.

The entire context of our meeting seemed bizarre. In a casual conversation at a party, a woman who said she was an astrologer – the first of her species I'd ever met – urged me to see Bloxham. I had heard of him but I confessed he had been so long out of the headlines, I thought he was dead. In fact, Arnall Bloxham was very much alive. He was a small man, white-haired and immaculately dressed with a rose in his buttonhole. His features were small, almost bird-like, with an impassivity that was quite Oriental. His voice and manner, quite precise, must have inspired confidence in his consulting room. Although nearly eighty years old he still treated numerous patients.

In Bloxham's rather lonely old house on the outskirts of Cardiff another middle-aged lady, a friend of Bloxham's, who said she was a 'psychic medium', served us tea. A little later, at Bloxham's rather amused bidding, she put her hand on my forehead, closed her eyes and pronounced that in previous incarnations I had once been a Moor and later a French alchemist. Both lives had ended violently!"

As a matter of fact, Iverson was not impressed. He wondered where he had landed.

"I shrugged it off. Mediums and all the para-phernalia of ouija boards and tealeaves have never fascinated me. At that stage, I was not very optimis-tic that Bloxham and his hypnosis would yield me very much. The setting heightened my impression of the oddity of the meeting. We sat in the hypno-tist's lounge, which has a handsome four-poster bed in which he sleeps, and on the wall a death mask of a nobleman said to have been murdered in that same bed. His hypnotist's couch was an ancient Welsh Bardic chair in carved oak. And Bloxham sat by a small antique table, piled high with tape recordings in neatly labelled boxes. When I asked him about them, he told me, very matter of fact, that over the previous twenty years he had tape-recorded over four hundred examples of reincarnation. Under repeated sessions of hypnosis some of his subjects had regressed to as many as fourteen quite separate existences spread out over centuries.

Now I had done some background reading, and I thought, if Bloxham's claim is true, then his tapes are possibly the largest investigation ever recorded into this phenomenon of regression under hypnosis. ...

He seemed an honest and balanced man, but it was a lot to take on trust. Then, as casually as if he were telling me where people had been for their holidays, he told me of an eye-witness account of the Great Fire of London in September 1666, and about someone who had lived in the Stone Age.

He played part of a tape in which a woman relived being a victim of the massacre of Jews in York in the twelfth century. Her agonized description of violence, fire and death of her daughter and herself was frankly hair-raising. But I accepted it as if I was listening to a very dramatic play – as yet I did not know about the historical background, the woman involved, or Arnell Bloxham.

But one name he mentioned decided me upon the next step. He said that years before he had hypnotized and regressed a young Press photographer named John Pike, who had made some outstanding television documentaries and completed tours of duty in Vietnam and Belfast. He was back in Cardiff and was not the sort of man I imagined would be much impressed with theories of reincarnation.

A few days later I was able to sit down and talk with him. Over a drink, he still recalled clearly his visit to the hypnotist's. Even though the tape-recording I subsequently listened to was dated 3rd October, 1957."

In his early days as a Press photographer, Pike went with a local reporter to visit Bloxham for a newspaper article about the supernatural. Bloxham, in his usual calm way, responded to their questions about reincarnation by suggesting a demonstration. First of all he hypnotized the reporter and tape-recorded a regression. And then he repeated the process with the photographer.

Pike recalled that the reporter had regressed to become a lawyer defending a country lad at an Assize court in England over a hundred years ago. The boy was found guilty of theft and sentenced to transportation. The 'lawyer' then became irritated with Bloxham's questions. First, the hypnotist was unfamiliar with the name of a noted judge of the time, and second, Bloxham apparently suggested that, because the sentence seemed harsh, the boy might appeal. 'Appeal', appeal, what is appeal?' was the angry response.

That was intriguing, because I soon found there had, in fact, never been any right to appeal under English law until the Judicature Acts of 1873. The 'lawyer' had been right. ...

But when it was Pike's turn to be hypnotized, he saw pictures and recalled events that puzzled him to this day. Recorded on tape, Pike becomes a wealthy farmer living near Kidderminster. He describes the clothes of the period, coins of the time he had in his purse, and how he eventually rode to London in the year 1649. In Whitehall, perched side-saddle on his horse, he saw, over the heads of a large crowd and Roundhead soldiers, the unfolding of a great historical event – the execution of King Charles I of England. John Pike remembers vividly that as the axe fell he shuddered and turned his eyes away.

Following the meeting with Pike, I revisited Bloxham and over a period of weeks heard, not without scepticism, tape-recordings of an astonishing variety of regressions.'

This clearly shows Iverson's rational and determined frame of mind. He then examined another chief witness – a married lady in her thirties whose regressions revealed seven former lives, and who, by coincidence, lived in the same area and had attended the same secondary school as he had. He arranged a meeting with her and heard that after the last regression she fainted and her husband called an end to any further regressions. This was five years earlier. Iverson then asked her whether she would be willing to have one more regression in front of the camera for a later TV documentary. She and her husband agreed, provided anonymity was observed.

Iverson was present at that event and remained a critical analyst throughout the work on this book.

Iverson selected from the 400 tapes mainly those relating to 'Jane Evans' and her seven lives. He checked all historical statements of names, dates and events against extant literature and consulted professors with specialist knowledge of a particular period. When relating the recordings he always pauses to add his historical references. This lends a particular authenticity to the text.

The most significant incarnation was that of a noble Roman woman, Livonia, living in Eboracum, the present York, in close friendship with Helena, the wife of the Governor. It was the year 286 AD when great events started to unfold. A pseudo delegate from Rome ordered the Governor Constantius back to Rome. In his absence, the delegate who had plotted with the admiral of the fleet to sever Britain from Rome wanted to take on the rule. All this caused great alarm among the noble ladies who for their own safety had to flee to Verulanum, the present St Albans. Livonia became a Christian and her husband, Titus, was to be ordained as a priest. But Diocletian, then Emperor, passed the edict that all Christians should be killed. This became the fate of husband and wife.

One extraordinary event is described from the earlier days in York: In their own garden, Titus gave instructions in the use of weaponry to Constantius's son, Constantine. This is the Constantine who later became Emperor of Rome and after whom the city of Constantinople received its name. He also introduced the toleration of Christianity in the Roman Empire.

Professor Hartley, an expert in the history of Roman Britain, listening to the tape, realized that there are gaps in the historical knowledge and that Livonia's story fitted very well into this existing gap.

Iverson's endeavour to find historical proof has yielded many positive results. And yet he applies still a question mark after the title 'More Lives Than One?' He, like so many 'rational' minds is under the spell of the image of the chain, which is only as strong as its weakest link. Is it not time to use Professor David Ray Griffin's image of the rope made up of many strands that still carries the weight, even though one strand or more might snap! Arnall Bloxham admits that memories can fail, as they can also in the present lifetime. This does not discredit the overall veracity of reincarnation. Magnus Magnusson, the renowned television broadcaster and journalist is more affirmative in his Foreword:

"In my years as a journalist and broadcaster, I have explored some very odd stories indeed... But the story told in this book must rank as the most intriguing story I've ever covered – because it contains all the elements of oddness and detective work and sheer strangeness that add up to a great mystery... But to me at least there is one incontrovertible conclusion – that the human mind is an infinitely more complex mystery and fascinating thing than we can even imagine." And further:

"The Bloxham Tapes – the most staggering evidence for reincarnation ever recorded."

K. O. Schmidt – fifty years of research as a Librarian

K. O. Schmidt deserves a special place in the context of this book. Facilitated by his profession, he collected from world literature many amazing stories of former lives remembered by different means. Friends and acquaintances also told many stories to him. The stories he relates are scrutinized and verified. His scope and insights are astounding and pre-date the research under hypnosis. In order to gain an impression of the scope of his work, the contents page of his book 'We Do Not Live Only Once' ('Wir Leben Nicht Nur Einmal') shall be given below:

Man, whence and whither? Recollection of former lives; The sudden nature of recollection; The circuit of births; Images of former lives; Earlier knowledge re-awakened; A pilgrimage through millennia; Causes of spontaneous remembrance; The case of Shanti Devi; Recollection by children; Return announced in advance; 'I have lived before'; The case of Katsugoro; Recollection in dream and trance; A report from Max Heindl; From the Wilson Collection; From the Shirley Collection; From the Brownell Collection; Appendix: The working of forces of destiny from life to life; The ledger of destiny; Causes of destiny; Words and deeds as factors causing destiny; Influences from former lives; The dynamics of destiny; Tasks of destiny research.

Considering that most chapters contain extensive examples of cases, one can gain some inkling of the impressive life's work of K. O. Schmidt. Unlike Iverson, he placed no question mark behind the title of his book. For him the veracity of his subject was beyond question. He based his judgement not only on the great names in history who were convinced of their previous lives, but also on the many testimonies he had collected, also of children remembering. Yet he was under no illusion regarding sceptics who would not accept anything but hard and fast 'facts'. In all recollection stories it is the individual concerned who accepts the lively nature of the experience with its identity character, which dispels all doubt: 'Thus I have been! So it is! This I have experienced!'

When some people discovered America, was it necessary for all Europeans to go there before acknowledging that America existed? Common sense can give an answer before the venerable institutions and conventions come up with their stamp of approval.

In the following I will recount one of the many stories the book contains:

A German teacher of languages was involved during the First World War in the battle of the Somme and, deeply affected by his experiences and despairing of his Christian faith, he turned to Eastern philosophy and yoga. Having learned about reincarnation he wanted to get his own experience. After advancing to the fourth grade of his exercises, where the soul detaches from the body to a certain extent, he returned with the vision of a gardener in a Scottish baronial estate. The butler then emerged from the castle, calling to the gardener, "Hello, Dudley!" At that moment it struck the teacher like lightning: "I am this Dudley!" It was the year 1587 and the castle was situated to the northwest of Edinburgh. The butler informed Dudley of the beheading of Mary Stuart and they both shared their fear that the Baron might be taken prisoner.

Years later the teacher wanted to catch a train at a Berlin station. It was very stormy and poured with rain. The street was empty and no taxi in sight. As he was about to meet the crossing of two roads he had a strange sensation as if something was about to happen. A few steps on he bumped into another man who also carried an umbrella. Both apologized, and doing so, they briefly looked at each other's strange face. As they parted, a strange feeling arose from the depth of the unconscious and a voice said: "You know him!"

He remembered having also seen some perplexed expression in the face of the stranger. He halted and looked back. The other man did the same and the teacher went back in spite of the torrential rain, and said, "excuse me, I have the feeling we know each other", and invited him into the nearby pub for a glass of wine. They were the only customers. They introduced themselves. The stranger was Dr Thomas, who described the strange feeling he had before turning the corner that something was about to happen. Dr Thomas was an art-historian. In a relaxed conversation he told of his hobby: he occupied himself with transcendental philosophy. In hours of deep contemplation he had come to the conclusion that he had been on earth many times before. In his inner vision he had seen himself in a past century in Mexico, northern France, at the Black Sea and in Scotland. From his last existence he knew that he served a baron northwest of Edinburgh as a butler during the reign of Queen Elizabeth I and Mary Stuart. He had then a special friend in whom he could trust and who was the head gardener of the estate. He always kept him informed of special events and once told him about the beheading of Mary Stuart. Spellbound the teacher listened to this story, having mentioned nothing of his own vision, and interrupted him with the question: 'Do you perhaps know the name of your former friend?' "Oh yes", he answered, "I know it perfectly well, he was called: James Dudley!"

As an example of the awakening of far-memories on journeys to foreign countries, from many similar stories, the following report by Friedrich Uhlemann of Oberhausen (Germany), which appeared in the periodical 'Wochenend', 171-51. (abridged):

"On my world travel in 1926 I came to Rio de Janeiro, where a brother in a monastery found me some work on a farm belonging to the monastery of St Bendo, close to Rio. There I became acquainted with a young man who invited me to meet his parent, living in the state of Santa Catarina, in a location called Blumenau. – I am a sober person, but experienced something strange there. On arrival I recognised the streets and squares and also the inscriptions on the crosses in the cemetery. The names were so familiar to me as if I had lived together with them, now dead. That this was not the case in this life is plain. – I cannot explain in any natural way the memories of this entirely unknown locality; neither have I any ancestors who have lived in this settlement."

K O Schmidt explains that "In poets, artists and philosophers, because of their greater sensitivity, far-memories occur more frequently than in people who are fully given up to their daily chores. The Swiss poet and statesman Heinrich Zschocke writes (an example for hundreds of others) that of all men he met in life there were only three of whom he knew for sure that he was related to in a former life. One of these was his wife; also she harboured similar memories of a relationship with him in a former life. – The Spanish painter, Salvador Dali, who paints dreamlike pictures with Christian symbolic tendencies, declared in an interview with the New York Herald Tribune (24.01.1960) "When you see my pictures, you will discover that one theme returns ever and again: the butterfly symbol of the soul: from the insignificant caterpillar – our bodily sheaths – the soul rises after death like a butterfly in all its beauty, freed from the earth … I am like many Spaniards, a mystic. But not that alone: I am a reincarnation of the Spanish mystic John of the Cross. I remember clearly my life as John, the life in the monastery and the many who lived together with me, the dark night of the soul and the experience of the unity with the divine" …

"If so many people remember details of former lives, why do not I ?", some readers will ask. – Conan Doyle, the author of the Sherlock-Holmes novels, who at the end of his life inclined towards spiritism, wrote in his book 'The History of Spiritism', an answer this question: "The flash of such remembrances could burden our present existence and complicate it severely and it would therefore be good that such memories should appear only when they might be necessary for our further development". – He speaks of a necklace of pearls which are united by the individuality. – Mahatma Gandhi is quoted as speaking about the blessing of not remembering, because life could become an unbearable burden if we would have to carry with us the abundance of sad memories. A wise man deletes willingly from his memory many things, as a judge, having dealt with the cases and details, forgets them.

Laura T. – a contemporary story

The following account is autobiographical and given to the author with the permission to publish. I consider it of great importance as an illustration for the countless horrendous sufferings and deaths that were inflicted and suffered during the last century and the present. They are carried as an unconscious burden in the present life. By recognising their origin, the dark legacy of the past can be shed through forgiving and genuine love in the present life.

"It was some five years ago that I had found a way of bringing myself into such a deep and relaxed state of mind that I could pluck into a level of consciousness where wisdom and clear intuition can be found. Being in that state, I did have contact with what I call 'guides', personae full of love, understanding and forgiveness that exist beyond the earthly realm of daily goings-on where perception is mostly blurred by unconscious thoughts and emotions. From that first moment on they supported and helped me find answers to the questions I had about issues of life and death and about current problems. They gave me comfort, patience, strength and anything I asked for, especially insights on how I can improve my life towards more balance and integrity.

At that particular time there was a specific challenge in my relationships that I found so hard to overcome, despite all the love and help my guides gave me. I decided to lay myself down and meditate and ask this question: 'The emotional pain I have right now is so overwhelming and in no proportion to the harm that has been done to me, that I wonder: Is there anything in a forgotten past that may have caused it?

During the meditation I got the answer: I identified with the life of a little Jewish girl in Amsterdam at the beginning of World War Two. The girl was living together with her whole family, grandparents included, in an apartment with blinded windows. Not being able to play with other children anymore, she suffered from loneliness and from the fact that her mother could hardly cope with the new situation where the Jews had to hide and where the father could no longer earn the money needed to feed so many people. Frustration and disbelief ruled and there were fights between the father and mother that made the insecurity of the outer world leak into their hidden home.

Nothing heart-breaking happened during that first meditation but I was tremendously agitated. Something moved me, made me shiver to the bone. I decided to carry on with it another time and see if I could explore this source of information in order to find a way out of the actual distress I felt in daily life.

But when I was ready to resume it, one of my guides stopped me! "Why would you want to seek a past life"? He asked. "Why would you not look for answer in your youth"? "Because it's these fragments about the girl, in Word War Two, that touched me very much. I am absolutely open to answers in more recent times, but the girl's life seems to be of great importance to me". Do you realise, he asked, that if you want to access your past life, you have to cross the border of death? Do you have the courage to do that?" "Can I bring somebody with me? I hesitated. "No, not a single thing or person. Even we will be invisible to you. We will stand by your side always, but you will not be able to notice us. The step through death is small and lasts only a short moment, but you will have to take it all by yourself. Are you ready"?

I was ready. He lead me into a dark tunnel at the end of which, I trusted, would be light. I knew that my courage and his support would lead me there in spite of unsuspected adventures. And courage was indeed needed because, although the start was rather uneventful, trauma after trauma was yet to come and be relived.

In a series of nine meditations, each lasting about three hours, the chain of the girl's life was linked together to the last minute of her life and beyond.

Roosje was her name, and she was an intelligent, very serious and shy child. Hunted by the Germans, the family fled from hiding place to hiding place, often splitting up, leaving the small child alone to face the terror of total insecurity in an unknown place with unknown people. When would her mum come back and take her back home to comfort her and explain what was going on? Some of her family rejoined, but not all: The tragedy of family members disappearing had begun. Roosje, her mother and her little brother were the only ones left when the train, on which they were loaded, departed to the first concentration camp.

It was there that life, little by little, turned out to be worse than hell. Humiliation and ill-treatment, hunger and dirt, rape after rape, medical experiments and sadism made the fragile butterfly of life seem less worth than the excrements filling the gutter in which the inhabitants of the camp had to defecate. How could one cope with so much suffering? Some people became indifferent; some turned mean. Some became listless and introvert, some showed their outrage but did not survive very long. Roosje's mother went crazy. She left her daughter all alone and only took care of her brother and herself. Roosje could not make sense of what was going on. How could a girl understand when a soldier who raped her regularly in exchange for, so-called, information about her beloved, lost father? What could she see in the fact that her mum got battered and scolded for trying to steal a loaf of bread for her starving children? How could she integrate the sentence she had to write down again and again in the camp school, 'The Jews are pigs' with her own experiences and self-image? Surely the Germans must be right in a way? Otherwise, why would their father have left them and why would they deserve such a horrible life if they essentially were not pigs indeed?

After two different camps and a very long march that cost many of the outworn lives of the prisoners, I realised that reliving Roosje's life would lead me to and through her death. Thank God I didn't do this alone. I would not have been able to. My guides were always with me and supported me, and explained how to deal with the things I saw. They would pick me out of scenes when they grew too horrible, to ease my nerves and to show me how to handle the overload of emotions. They taught me countless lessons about life and death, about sadism and the cost of ignorance, about compassion and forgiveness of the soul, who was not able to be cleansed of the bloodstains of such cruel experiences, and therefore tended to feel guilty for what she had attracted. Does it sound illogical, that a suffering soul needs forgiveness, even if it was not her fault? But that is exactly what she needs to be able to be healed: Unending love and forgiveness.

My guides showed me what had happened after Roosje got finally shot on the edge of a self-dug mass grave: She didn't accept the fact of her death and wandered around amidst so many other lost spirits, looking for her little brother and crying for her mum. 'What would you need to be able to accept this death'? They asked me, after having taken me away from the desolate scene. "but I can't", I replied. "There is no way that I can accept what has happened". "What prevents you"? 'I wanted to live. I wanted to prove that life was worth living. I wanted to grow up and do things, make life beautiful. I refuse to accept that people can really do such things to each other."

"So you cannot accept that things were, as they were, and that people were as you have experienced them"? "That's right". "You understand that there is a difference between accepting as acknowledging and accepting as agreeing? You could acknowledge what has happened, even if you don't approve of it". "I see". "And do you realise that you cannot lead a life as Laura a hundred percent, as long as you have not said goodbye to the life of Roosje? You will always partly be her, with all of her unfinished business bubbling under the surface, leading you to act and think and feel, not as Laura, but as Roosje, for reasons far away and no longer relevant". "I understand." "First yield to Roosje's life and death, and then release her and yourself. Practise this during the coming weeks. Next time you will be ready".

I could hardly believe it possible to find peace on the background of Roosje's life. But with the help of my guides I succeeded. Yielding to Roosje's death, paradoxically, made those last minutes very intense and more living than ever: The grip of the hand of the old man next to her – may God help his soul – I will always be grateful for the deep love in his eyes, just before his arms and legs were sent into a spasm by the blast of the gun. Endless seconds after that, the heart of the soldier standing opposite seemed to explode into a star of light, sending the bullet that would cut the last thread of Roosje's life. Death comes not in one moment. Death turns out to be a decision. The helpers from the other side needed some time to talk me into leaving the abused and wasted body behind.

And there was light, and there were my beloved helpers, and even some of my grandparents, who had passed away long ago, to congratulate and hug me. They sent me back to Laura's life, to live it, to love and grieve, to be upset, be disappointed or disorientated, in short: to honestly feel all the feelings that life imposes on us, with mildness towards ourselves.

Have I changed through this experience? Absolutely! Some things were different from one day to the next: I understood the deep disgust of uniforms, my distrust of men in general and my fear of sexual harassment. The connection to my parents changed tremendously, and so did my relationships. But most of all changed the perception of myself. For the first time in my life I felt grounded, I felt completely to be Laura, and this river of unending grief that I had always experienced to be flowing over the bottom of my soul, had finally vanished. I cannot even begin to describe how much I have learned from this experience, thanks to the unconditional help of my guides. I will always be grateful to them for all eternity."

Chapter 3

Children Remember their Former Life

Dr Ian Stevenson – fifty years' research into children who remember their former lives

The Pioneer of Reincarnation Research

A reprint from the internet.

"Dr Ian Stevenson was a former head of the Department of Psychiatry at the University of Virginia, and then the Director of the Division of Perpetual Studies at the University of Virginia. He has devoted the last 40 years to the scientific documentation of past life memories of children from all over the world and has over 3000 cases in his files. Many people, including sceptics and scholars, agree that these cases offer the best evidence yet for reincarnation.

Dr Stevenson's research into the possibility of reincarnation began in 1960 when he heard of a case in Sri Lanka where a child claimed to remember a past life. He thoroughly questioned the child and the child's parents, as well as the people whom the child claimed were his parents from a past life. This led to Dr Stevenson's conviction that reincarnation was possibly a reality. The more cases he pursued, the greater became his drive to scientifically open up and conquer an unknown territory among the world's mysteries, which until now had been excluded from scientific observation. Nonetheless, he believed he could approach and possibly furnish proof of its reality with scientific means.

In 1960, Dr Stevenson published two articles, in the Journal of the American Society for Psychical Research, about children who remembered past lives. In 1974, he published his book, 'Twenty Cases suggestive of Reincarnation', and became well known, wherever his book appeared, by those people who already had a long-standing interest in this subject. They were pleased to finally be presented with such fundamental research into reincarnation from a scientific source. In 1997, Dr Stevenson published his work entitled 'Reincarnation and Biology'. In the first volume he mainly describes birthmarks – those distinguishing marks on the skin, which the newborn baby brings into the world and cannot be explained by inheritance alone. In his second volume, Dr Stevenson focussed mainly on deformities and other abnormalities that children are born with and which cannot be traced back to inheritance, prenatal, or perinatal (created during birth) occurrences. This monumental piece of work contains hundreds of pictures documenting the evidence.

During his original research into various cases involving children's memories of past lives, Dr Stevenson did note with interest the fact that these children frequently bore lasting birthmarks, which supposedly related to their murder, or death, they suffered in a previous life. Stevenson's research into birthmarks and congenital defects has such particular importance for the demonstration of reincarnation, superior to the often fragmentary memories and reports of the children and adults questioned which, even if verified afterwards, cannot be assigned the same value in scientific terms.

In many cases presented by Dr Stevenson there are also medical documents available as further proof, which are usually compiled after the death of the person. Dr Stevenson adds that in the cases he researched and "solved" in which birthmarks and deformities were present, he didn't suppose there was any other apposite explanation than that of reincarnation. Only 30% – 60% of these deformities can be put down to birth defects which related to genetic factors, viral infections or chemical causes (like those of Thalidomide or alcohol). Apart from these demonstrable causes, the medical profession has no other explanation of why a person is born with these deformities and why they appear precisely in that part of their body and in no other.

Most of the cases where birthmarks and congenital deformities exist have one to five characteristics in common.

(1) In the most unusual scenario, it is possible that someone who believed in reincarnation expressed a wish to be reborn to a couple or one partner of a couple. This is usually because they are convinced that they would be well cared for by those particular people. The Tlingit Indians of Alaska and the Tibetans often make these requests.

(2) More frequent than this are the prophetic dreams. Someone who has died appears to a pregnant

or not as yet pregnant woman and tells her that he or she will be reborn to her. Sometimes relatives or friends have dreams like this and will then relate the dream to the mother to be. Dr Stevenson found these kinds of dreams to be particularly prolific in Burma and among the Indians of Alaska.

(3) In these cultures the body of a newborn child is checked for recognizable marks to establish whether the deceased person they had known is reborn to them. This search for marks of identification is very common in cultures that believe in reincarnation, and especially among the Tlingit Indians and the Igbos of Nigeria. Various tribes of West Africa make marks on the body of the recently deceased in order to be able to identify the person when he or she is reborn.

(4) The most frequently occurring event or common denominator relating to rebirth is probably that of a child remembering a past life. Children usually begin to talk about their memories between the ages of two and four. Such infantile memories gradually dwindle when the child is between four and seven years old. There are, of course, always some exceptions, such as a child continuing to remember its previous life, but not speaking about it for various reasons.

Most children talk about their previous identity with great intensity and feeling. Often they cannot decide for themselves which world is real and which one is not. They often experience a kind of double existence where at times one life is more prominent, and at times the other life takes over. This is why they usually speak of their past life in the present tense saying things like, "I have a husband and two children who live in Jaipur." Almost all of them are able to tell us about the events leading up to their death.

Such children tend to consider their previous parents to be their real parents rather than their present ones, and usually express a wish to return to them. When the previous family has been found and details about the person in that past life have come to light, then the origin of the fifth common denominator – the conspicuous or unusual behaviour of the child – is becoming obvious.

(5) For instance, if the child is born in India to a very low-class family and was a member of a higher caste in the previous life, it may feel uncomfortable in its new family. The child may ask to be served and waited on hand and foot and may refuse to wear cheap clothes.'

Stevenson gives us several examples of these unusual behaviour patterns: in 35% of cases he investigated, children who died an unnatural death developed phobias. For example, if they had drowned in a past life then they frequently developed a phobia about going out of their depth in water. If they had been shot, they were often afraid of guns and, sometimes, loud bangs in general. If they died in a road accident they would sometimes develop a phobia of travelling in cars, buses and lorries.

Another frequently observed unusual form of behaviour, which Dr Stevenson called 'philias', concerns children who express the wish to eat different kinds of food or to wear clothes that were different from those of their culture. If a child had developed an alcohol, tobacco or drug addiction as an adult in a previous incarnation he may express a need for these substances and develop certain cravings at an early age.

Many of these children with past-life memories show abilities or talents that they had in their previous lives. Often children who were members of the opposite sex in their previous life show difficulty in adjusting to the new sex. These problems relating to 'sex change' can lead to homosexuality later on in their lives. Former girls who were reborn as boys may wish to dress as girls or prefer to play with girls rather than boys.

Until now all these human oddities have been a mystery to conventional psychiatrists – after all, parents could not be blamed for their children's behaviour in these cases. At least research into reincarnation is shedding some light on the subject. In the past, doctors blamed such peculiarities on a lack or a surplus of certain hormones, but now they will have to do some rethinking." …

These last observations by Dr Stevenson point to the study of karma. One of the laws of karma is that past problems appear again to be dealt with, and shortcomings to be overcome in the present life. They should not therefore remain just a fact or excuse, similar to a genetic disposition, but rather be a developmental challenge!

Jenny Cockell – who found her 'Yesterday's Children'

Jenny Cockell's book appeared in 1993 under the title 'Yesterday's Children'. Her Foreword ends with the words: "It's hard to be certain where my story starts – it's not really with my childhood or even my birth. In a sense it starts with Mary's death. But of one thing I am sure, it would never have happened without the dream…"

As a young child Jenny dreamt of Mary, who died alone in an Irish hospital, worried for the seven children she would leave behind. During day she also remembered other situations from Mary's life.

Her Mother was the only one who listened to her, others dismissed her 'fancies' and she became rather remote and introvert, left alone with her inner realities.

In her early years she drew simple maps of Mary's village and her house. She knew for certain, it was in Ireland. All the memories came to her like pieces of a jigsaw puzzle, but she felt an inner certainty that together they would make a whole.

In her book she writes: "I have always known that the period of time involved was roughly 1898 to the 1930s that was the span of Mary's life."

The child tried to identify Mary's village on a map of Ireland: 'Each time I was drawn back to the same spot… called Malahide, and it was just north of Dublin'.

However real these memories were to Jenny, she

had to find out again and again that this was not the case for other people.

In Sunday school the talk was about life and death and she felt disappointed that nothing was said about former lives. On that day she discovered that reincarnation was considered a belief and not a fact, therefore not generally accepted in Britain. The discovery that it was only her truth and that she was different, was a great shock to her – because grown-ups are usually right.

When she was eight years old she realised that premonitions she had were proved right which gave her confidence that her memories were right too, even though people did not share them.

She could not understand why other children found inconsequential things so important. So she remained an outsider during all her childhood and adolescence, never feeling completely integrated.

The unhappy home situation, after experiencing years of fear, ended with the divorce of the parents. This even aggravated her condition. But beyond all daily miseries she clung to the tentative wish that one day she might find the cottage and find the answer to her torment about the seven children. Only her Mother knew about her secret wish as only she knew about 'Mary'.

Jenny had to cope with hard times whilst her mother studied for qualifications and gained professional competence and found employment. School was overshadowed by the present and the past and only when attending college she achieved what would prepare her for the future.

Destiny was kind to her by finding an understanding and supportive husband. When she herself became a mother she found a new understanding for the urge, which Mary felt, as the connection to her children. The wish to visit Ireland arose again, but money was scarce.

Yet the day came when, during a weekend and cheap flight she was able to visit Dublin and Malahide. She felt vindicated that her dreams and memories were real. She found enough evidence to verify the correctness of the map she had drawn as a child. Yet the cottage was there no more. The neighbouring farmer, however, remembered the cottage and the family that once lived there in the 20s and 30s of the last century.

Then began a period for Jenny in which she advanced her quest more forcefully. She started contacting people without hesitation and wrote letters with more confidence and purpose. Many inner and outer obstacles had to be faced till at last she even put a request for information about the family into Dublin newspapers.

In the course of her search she also made her acquaintance with a TV journalist who wanted to be helpful. But the lack of photographic evidence postponed this approach to a later date.

Another contact was made with a hypnotist, a past-life therapist. She refused any performance in public, but agreed, however, to being regressed in a small ladies' circle. It is of interest to note some of the experiences she described. She experienced hypnotic regression as double-edged, wonderful and disturbing at the same time. Some memories are rightfully pushed into the deep recesses of the 'mind' – the soul – for a good reason and self-protection. By exposing deep memories, the individual is forced to look at both – the forgotten and the repressed.

These regressions added certain details to what Jenny knew anyway but yielded no answers to essential questions she had. 'I was drifting between the two personalities. I was instructed to look into the official register and give a name and date, which appeared with unlikely clarity. The name given was O'Neil, and the date was 1921. I was not at all sure that these were correct.'

Later she found out through ordinary research that the family name was Sutton.

The hypnotist was interested in understanding or proving the continuity of the 'soul', whilst Jenny was anxious to discover more details of her lost family. She therefore felt that regression either produced 'too much or not enough'. She experienced it 'like an addiction' and that 'time became her enemy'. The feeling of a Pandora's Box remained. She notes 'The intensity of remembering under hypnosis left me feeling opened up, raw, vulnerable and confused. There was a tremendous conflict between self-preservation and the needs from the past'. It was traumatic.

Certain 'stupid' questions filled her with anger and 'the level of irritation' was rising. She did not want to know of her former personalities in France and Wales. She wanted to find Mary's children and felt there were too much conflict of interest between her and the hypnotist and she therefore terminated future sessions.

Jenny Cockell's need for proof and her search were more emotional than rational. She knew that Mary's children could be age-wise her parents. She was born 21 years after Mary's death, and the oldest child, a boy, was then thirteen.

The search went on. She made a second visit to Malahide, made new contacts, found more evidence and confirmation. Jenny devised questionnaires for newspapers and magazines, for historical societies and recording offices and now equipped with the family name she approached a Catholic priest and director of orphanages as part of the Department of Education in Dublin.

At last she received a list of the whole family, John Sutton and his wife Mary nee Hand and the six names with the year of their birth: three sons and three daughters together with the names of their married partners. (One child had died).

The priest's reply was wonderfully positive, constructive and considerate. He accepted this 'extraordinary phenomenon' as the hand of God, and it was a great confirmation to Jenny. In 1990 a copy of the death certificate was sent to her.

First on Jenny's mind was now to find Mary's children. A surprise letter arrived in response to Jenny's publicity efforts; it came from the daughter of one of the sons. Also a phone-call came: the caller was interested to know what connection she had to the family and she had to explain: I know it's going to sound strange, but I remember the family through dreams'. Despite some confusion on the other end of the line, she was given more details, addresses and phone numbers.

The three sons had had a re-union a few years before, but with the sisters the contact was lost. For Jenny Cockell an emotional adjustment was needed, now that a first contact with members of the family was made. The welfare of the family was her overriding goal.

As no further response came from the second son she decided to phone the first son who lived in England. After some harrowing delays she was able to visit him after a three hours' journey. Jenny was greatly excited to meet this man, old enough to be her father! A television reporter had been a go-between and had compiled a list of comparisons. They compared the notes and discussed them point-by-point. The concept of her 'memories', being so accurate, was quite new to him and he received each revelation about his childhood with enthusiasm and wonder. 'How could anyone know so much about his private world?' He showed her photographs of his brothers and filled in many more details.- The best thing about meeting Sonny, apart from getting to know a lovely person, was finding out at last what had happened to Mary's family.

—⁓—

It would go beyond the frame of this amazing story to follow each of Mary's children in detail.

Jenny Cockell's efforts resulted in facilitating the still living members of Mary's family to get in touch with each other. The helpful priest, to whom the idea of reincarnation was taboo, blessed Jenny for having been sent by God to unite the family again.

A television show, presenting Jenny Cockell and

Mary's eldest son, came about at a later date where the presenter questioned them.

This story is so unique because the particularly short time of rebirth was so obviously influenced by Mary's great concern of having left her children orphaned and by the faithful determination of Jenny Cockell to finding 'yesterday's children' again.

Barbro Karlen – remembering Life as Anne Frank

From Dennis Eisenberg in Stockholm reprinted in The Express, 28th March, 2000

"A woman who claims to be the reincarnation of Anne Frank has finally broken her silence after a lifetime of torment reliving the ordeal of the young Jewish diarist who hid from the Nazis in the Second World War.

Barbro Karlen's secret was first accepted by her parents when she was 10 years old. Eight years before, when she had barely begun to speak, their daughter had first insisted: "I have another name. It's Anne Frank. I want to go home."

When the Karlen family travelled from their Gothenburg home in Sweden to Amsterdam, scene of Anne's hiding place, she immediately declared: "I feel I'm at home here". Next morning the family visited the house where the Frank family hid until they were sent to Bergen-Belsen concentration camp, where Anne died of typhus.

Unsure of the address, Barbro's father was about to hail a taxi, when his daughter told him:

"I know exactly where the house is. We can easily walk there. It's not very far".

Barbro told the Express: "I recognised the house immediately although I had never seen a picture of it before. I knew in my heart and my soul that this was the house I had lived in".

That was 33 years ago. After a lifetime in which Barbro has relived the horror of Anne's deportation to a concentration camp she has written a book about her amazing double life: 'The Wolves Howled: Fragments of Two Lifetimes', was published in Britain (April 2000).

Barbro, 43, says the first time her parents accepted that she was the reincarnation of Anne Frank was when they followed her into the tiny secret annex where the Frank family had hidden. Barbro cried out in anguish when she noticed that pictures of Hollywood stars, which Anne had put on the wall, had gone. A guide confirmed to her parents that they had been taken away for framing.

"It was at that moment that I saw from the look on the faces of my parents that both of them finally believed me totally that I had not been fantasising," she said.

My father told me, "I know that we had never taken you to Amsterdam. None of us have even seen a photograph of this house. It must have been in a different life that you were here. There can be no other explanation."

But the experience was overpowering for Barbro, who "grew increasingly terrified. My whole body was shaking and the tears were pouring down my face".

She added: "I just had to get out of that house. As I came down the stairs I sensed that a man in a green uniform was going to try and kill me. For the last 35 years of my life I saw that uniformed man again and again in my nightmares". Barbro is convinced she had sensed the storm trooper who took Anne off to Belsen.

When she was four, her mother took her to a psychiatrist who said: "She's perfectly normal. She will grow out of it." But the similarities with Anne Frank, the gifted Dutch writer, are uncanny. When Barbro was 11 a family friend chanced to walk into her bedroom when she was at school and was astonished to find manuscripts scattered on chairs.

Barbro had written short stories, essays, poems and philosophic dissertations dealing with life and death. She was hailed as a child prodigy and hit the best-seller list in Sweden. But she stayed silent about her reincarnation belief and joined the police "to try to cure myself of the phobia of uniforms."

Later she had to quit. "It was at that stage that all my half-suppressed life as being Anne Frank suddenly crashed through into my conscious thoughts again," she said. "My dreams of what happened to her in the concentration camp grew ever more vivid." It was Barbro's realisation "that I had been given the gift of writing as Anne Frank had been so blessed" that helped her cope. "I knew that I had to write down every single thing which happened", she said.

"Having completed the book I have finally found peace and accept my situation as a fact of life. I felt I had to write and tell the world about the evil of the slaughter of the Jews in the Holocaust. As Barbro Karlen I was given the chance of doing something about it, which I was not able to do in my past life. The purpose of the book was not to prove that I was Anne Frank, nor to ask if you believe in reincarnation. It is to pass on the message which has taken me over 40 years to understand: To appreciate the awe and profundity of life"."

An interview with Barbro Karlén for New View magazine, (summer issue 2000).

By Tom Raines

Born in Sweden in 1954, Barbro Karlén was haunted during her childhood by horrific dreams and memories of her life as Anne Frank, the young Jewish girl who had died in a German Concentration camp and who later became famous throughout the world when her diary was published. Barbro herself became famous in Sweden when, at the age of 12, she had a book of poems published which became the bestselling poetry book of all time in Sweden. By the age of 17 she had published ten works of poetry and prose. When Clairview Books (an imprint of Temple Lodge Publishing) was launched, offering works to the public sharing people's spiritual experiences, they chose to include, translated from the Swedish original, Barbro Karlén's book 'And the Wolves Howled'. The book is basically an autobiography, containing her struggles to come to terms with her appalling memories. Barbro worked for18 years as a mounted policewoman in Sweden and has trained and competed in dressage for over 30 years. Her book includes the story of her damaging persecution in Sweden by those who she eventually understood as being her tormentors in her previous life as Anne Frank. Yet, in this life, she has overcome this adversity. The following interview took place in April when Barbro Karlén was in London to publicise her book.

I understand that many years before writing your book you had made a decision not to speak about your experiences. Is this because you felt that you would be misunderstood?

I did not realise then the big importance of being brave enough to write my story. I thought that maybe I would shock people with it. Also, the relatives of Anne Frank who were still living might be hurt by it. I couldn't see what good my speaking openly about these things would bring to the world. I could not see that it was meant for me to talk about this. I was so damaged by all that I had been through in Sweden and I could not think about opening myself up to more attacks. [Barbro was accused and vilified in the Swedish press of cruelty to her horses and the book charts her struggles to stand up against this and clear her name.] When I was growing up it was natural to talk about my memories. Yet as I grew older I came to realise that I should not talk about it, my parents were very upset about it, quite disturbed, they did not believe in reincarnation. So I realised it was better for me to be quiet. Since the dreams did not leave me,

I still had my memories and had to get them out in some way, so I started to write. My writings were 'discovered' and ten books were published in five years. I never wrote about my memories concerning Anne Frank, but I wrote about reincarnation in different ways, weaving it into my stories. Around the age of eight or nine, my teacher at school began to talk about Anne Frank. I was so astonished at how she could tell me something that I had known for my whole life. I heard the story and then realised that Anne Frank was a famous person who had written this diary. When my teacher spoke about Anne Frank's life, some I knew was right, but some of it I didn't agree with. But I could never speak up and say anything, I just had to sit quiet. I just wanted to forget about it, not talk about it. I was just happy that I had my writing.

Was there ever a time when you didn't believe in reincarnation?

No, it would have been like denying my childhood. My memories were so clear from my childhood, both in my dreams and my daily life, of the events and the terror which Anne Frank went through.

Do you feel that inside you are two personalities?

No. Rather as a child I felt I lived in two worlds. Every night I had these fearful dreams and would wake up crying and afraid. Then I would be awake in a secure home with loving parents where all was well. The dreams and memories were one world and my life as Barbro another. It was confusing for me.

Did you have any experiences during the day, like flashes of consciousness, taking you into another world?

No. Not before I came to Anne Frank's house in Amsterdam when I was ten years old. [When Barbro was ten she and her parents made a visit to Amsterdam. To her parent's astonishment, Barbro was able to lead them to the street and the house where Anne Frank had lived, and was able to tell them what they would find inside.] But since then I have not had other experiences like that, only in my dreams. Around the age of 15 the dreams began to fade away and become more vague. They slowly drifted away from me and for this I was deeply grateful and happy. I could now really live my own life. The writing, which had been a great help to me as a means of expressing myself, also receded. It did not stop altogether but went more into the background.

You mention in your book your strong memories of men in uniforms dragging you, as Anne Frank, away, and that you went into the police force to get rid of this fear of uniforms, to consciously confront your fear?

Yes. When I was a child I could hide behind my mother, but as an adult I found I was still wanting to escape and run away from the police when, say, they wished to check my driver's license. I could not control this phobia. Joining the police was a solution for me. When I first put on the uniform, it was one of the most terrifying experiences of my life. I have likened it in my book to being afraid of spiders and then someone throws a bucket of them over you and they crawl over you, in your hair, in your mouth, everywhere and you can't get them off. That was how I felt. I was terrified but came through it. It served its purpose and after a while I no longer thought about it.

Was this the only reason to join the police?

I had three reasons. Fear of uniforms was one, but I was also joining the mounted police and as a horse rider it was lovely to be paid for something I enjoyed so much. Also I was a single parent at the time, with insufficient income and I needed a job.

Why were horses so important you?

Probably because I was so lonely as a child. I liked all animals, but there is a special communication between a rider and a horse that cannot be compared to anything else. It was such a relief for me to be able to ride such a creature. It is like a mind reading thing between the horse and yourself.

Did this empathy in thinking with a horse help ease in any way the terror of your memories of Anne Frank?

When I am riding I seem to forget everything around me and that is a moment akin to meditation – all thoughts clear out of your head. For me that is a most wonderful thing.

In the book, you describe a certain persecution you went through with the press and other people, maligning you for how you treated horses. The book ends without saying what happened in your efforts to clear your name through the courts. Has there been an outcome?

I hope to write a sequel to 'And the Wolves Howled' and tell further what happened. Also to try and tell more about my thoughts on reincarnation, the reason why I wrote this present book and the theory of why I was able to have my memories of Anne Frank. Concerning the legal situation, it has proved very difficult to bring a process through the courts. Many obstacles appeared in the way. Justice seems a long way off. Eventually I appealed to the High Court. It took over one and a half years to get a date for a hearing. Then two weeks before the hearing one of the witnesses for my accusers, a journalist, said she could not attend, she was away in New York. So it was postponed, another date set, again postponed. Then I received notification, with a certificate, that one of my accusers, a woman, is now mentally ill so the hearing has been indefinitely cancelled. It is like fighting shadows. Whilst it remains important for me to obtain justice, I feel that writing this book and telling my story is giving me justice by another way, no matter what happens through the courts. I do not feel threats from them any longer, I feel that they cannot hurt me any more.

So what theory do you wish to share with the world through writing another book on reincarnation?

The reason I wrote this current book was not to prove that I was Anne Frank, there is no point to try to do that. Yet I could not write this book without talking about my memories. I would have been much happier if they had been memories from another life, not a well-known person. But the important thing is that I wanted to write about the connection between the lives. In this life someone may be suffering from the events of their life and if I can plant a little seed in their head or heart which says "maybe I am so weird with this and that or maybe this is happening to me because of what happened to me in a former lifetime. Or because I have to learn from what is happening to me now in order to cope with something to come in another lifetime". That might then help people who are having a difficult time. There are people today on medication or shut up in hospitals because they have some behavioural problems which might be solved if they could hear about the possibility of reincarnation. I think it important that people are open minded for reincarnation. Maybe some time in the future, even the near future, reincarnation will no longer be a fiction for many people but a fact and imagine how that would change the world. Imagine if the leaders of the world realised that what they are doing is not only for the next generation, but that they have to come back and face the consequences of their actions again.

In your book you mention two experiences, separated by perhaps thirty years. Both occur when you are on a beach looking out to sea. The first is when as a child you experience a transcendental moment, experiencing the love, peace and communion with everything and then recognising a yearning inside of yourself to have someone you could share your difficult memories and experiences with. You write that you then 'saw' footprints wandering in the sand and followed them and came in the presence of this 'wanderer'. This being standing before you was "Everything you had looked for" and he said to you; "Perhaps I am not always visible to people when I am close to you, but I shall always be in you and with you". Then, he is gone from your sight as you become conscious again of your normal world. Towards the end of your book you describe a second experience. How, at the end of your strength in the seemingly futile battle to clear your name and salvage a life that is all but destroyed [for Barbro had lost much during this time and the horrific dreams of what happened to her as Anne Frank had returned] you again find yourself by the sea, remembering the 'Wanderer'. How, following in his footsteps and the meeting together had remained with you over the years. You go on to describe how you then, on the beach, searched again for his closeness and perfection. You share how the setting of the sun and the beauty of nature and her creatures at twilight brought you the grace of peace and a new strength to go on with your life. Out of this experience comes the decision to write the book. Can you say more about this?

At the end of the book I speak about going to the beach and finding a piece of God inside myself. But then the dreams started again, yet whereas always before they had been terrifying, now they came with a peace. In the dreams, a room had always held terror for me because I was locked in, but now I felt I could leave whenever I wanted to. In my dreams, in this room, I saw myself writing this book, I was looking over the shoulder of myself as Anne Frank. The picture shifted, so that sometimes I was looking over the shoulder of Anne Frank and sometimes I was looking over the shoulder of myself looking as I do in this life. That was the first time I was ever 'looking' at myself from outside. It was as if I was my higher self looking over the shoulder. Always in the earlier memories I was 'inside' and the events were happening to me. Here I was looking from the outside, observing.

Was this the first dream after the beach?

Yes.

Was that first experience on the beach, when you were a child, what some might call a Christ experience?

I would say it was Christ, perhaps in the light of my upbringing in a Christian, rather than religious, home. The naming of it does not matter, it is the force of the spirit that is God. After the second experience at the beach, when the dreams began again, I 'read' the book as it was being written in the dream, looking over 'my' shoulder. And when I woke in the morning my head was full of sentences and all these words – 1 had to write it all down.

Did you write exactly what you 'read' in your dream?

I have a feeling I wrote exactly what I experienced in my dreams. There were so many words that wanted to come out of the pen. I was writing in the 'I' form [first person singular] and when I had written a couple of chapters it was so close to me, taking over my life somehow, that I had to stop for a moment and find another way to cope with it. Then I decided to write the book as if writing about someone else [in the book she calls the main character Sarah, rather than her own name, Barbro], making it a little more distant.

So you then wrote the book, like the dream, looking in at the situation 'over the shoulder' so to speak.

Yes, I had not thought of it like that, but that is true.

Have you had other distinct spiritual experiences in your life?

No, and I do not remember any other 'lives' that I have lived. Although, as a child I could sometimes see danger, an event, before it happened. It occurred rarely but when it did it was very clear.

Did people listen to your warnings?

Yes, I was around ten or eleven. It only happened a few times.

What is your earliest memory?

When I was about four and a half, riding on my father's shoulders.

You write in the book that when you were two, your mother said that you told her your name was Anne …

She never told me about this until much later. They did not believe in what I was saying when I was young. But after the visit to Amsterdam and the house of Anne Frank my Mother was convinced. My Father also, although he was totally against reincarnation. He still did not want to talk about it. He believed me, but said I must be the only one reincarnated. He did not want to accept this truth.

Did he ever change his attitude?

Towards the end of his life he came closer to this.

Since your Mother died last year, has anything changed in you?

It was a deep trauma for me. I was always afraid of her death because we were very close. After the experience in the house in Amsterdam it was like we shared a secret. I am also an only child. She was 36 and married for ten years before I was born. So we were very close. She was always there for me. She was progressively ill for the last years of her life and so I was able to get used to her going gradually. At the end she came out of the hospital and 1 nursed her at home. It was what we both wanted. After her death I felt her very close to me, closer somehow than when she was alive. I feel now she is free of her body she is really helping me. I gain a lot of strength from this.

How is your dream life now?

Quite normal, I am happy to say!

Is there a question you would wish to be asked?

One is, what do I want to achieve with the book and being interviewed by the press – what would I do with it? Some people might think I'm doing this to get famous, rich etc. I do not seek fame. I had this when I was young as an author and hated it then. Yet I realise that being well known enables me to get a message across to more people. And it is important that people are listening, because I want to talk about reincarnation. When I think about people today and the new millennium, what we are coming into, I find people are losing more and more the spirit they have inside themselves – their connection to nature, to God and themselves. I think that in the new time we are coming into, people need to come into a more private relation to God. Not to have these churches and different religions where people are fighting each other and having to belong to a religious community in order to be allowed to come into God's Kingdom. This is something I dream of and perhaps it sounds naive, but to have places all over the world where people can come, whatever their religious background, knowing that they have a force for good in them, and to feel that goodness no matter whether they believe in God or not, reincarnation or not, but that they want to fight for the good force and to fight against evilness – that would be something I would dream of. If it was possible to create such places – free from separated religion and icons. A new start for a new humanity. Maybe the last chance for human beings to come to their senses.

What you describe seems to be an open 'Church'. Don't people need something they share in common in order to work with one another – to learn to sit down with one another, in spite of differences, with good will?

That Higher Spirit that I found helps us to do this. Each of us has a Higher Spirit. It is how we are in our soul and how we act to ourselves and the people around us, towards strangers.

Do you hope that the struggles in your life can inspire others to connect to a higher reality in life, to the truth of their lives?

That is how I feel, although I sometimes feel so limited. There are so many things I want to share to give and to tell about.

Where does this all spring from?

From the inner soul. In the beginning was good and evil. The good started life, the flame. Evilness puts black into this. When we live our lives, one time after time, good and evil fight in us. It is our task to aid the good. That is our responsibility.

Do you think evil can be transformed?

I think so. If the power is strong enough from enough souls it is possible to turn the evil around. That is the hope that we must have.

Thank you, Barbro Karlén.

Rabbi Yonassan Gershom
– beyond the ashes

Rabbi Yonassan Gershom 'Beyond the Ashes, Cases of Reincarnation from the Holocaust'

This is a most remarkable collection of children's stories remembering the Holocaust. Rabbi Gershom had become a strong magnet for people to come forward to tell him their own story.

Gershom comes from the Hasidic tradition of Judaism where reincarnation is accepted as a fact of life. He is a counsellor, lecturer and writer and known and respected in western countries.

His book is not just a collection of remembered stories by reincarnated victims of the Holocaust, he is also a profound thinker and interpreter of the Jewish faith. He is well informed about the spiritual existence of the human being, both in this world and that of the spirit, the Bardo, the realm of the soul-spirit's sojourn between incarnations. He speaks with authority from his point of view on many allied questions. Through his counselling and widely read literature, he has gained deep insights into the working of karma.

He is familiar with the works of Edgar Cacey, Dr Ian Stevenson, Dr Joel Whitton and others.

With thoughtful and empathetic interest he counselled those who entrusted their memories to him. He was himself surprised at the short intervals between death and rebirth in the case of the majority of these children. He believes that they made up the post-war baby boom of the 40s and 50s. Jewish souls were frequently reborn into non-Jewish families and often experienced themselves as strangers, or were experienced as such. Fear was often a driving force that brought a soul back into life where they had to learn to overcome fear. The counsellor had to become a healer. Jews only later on were allowed to speak of their own feelings. Gershom speaks of the souls of around a million children born again very soon. They also brought with them a common resolve: to change the treatment of children. No more physical punishment and fear-inspiring threats and stories. Children should experience love and respect and a gentle approach. Much of mainstream changes were, unknowingly, brought about by children reborn from the Holocaust!

Gershom describes the ethnic minority of Jewry as peaceful and non-violent. His teacher Reb Zalman, came up with the comparison between the suffering of Jews throughout the ages and the white blood corpuscles sacrificing themselves for the body, threatened by infection, and the body of mankind, being saved by the sacrifice of Jewish lives. Many modern Jews would not subscribe to this idea!

Again to the children: Certain impressions caused irrational fears: black jackboots and barbed wire; enclosed rooms or showers. Victims in the camps were told they would go to the shower, which proved to be a gas chamber. Many such experiences were appearing in dreams and spontaneous memories. Gershom stresses that all his many 'anecdotes' do not amount to scientific proof; he had to deal with souls who had come to him for help. But surely these stories add to the strands of the 'rope' mentioned in 'More Than One Life'!

The later chapters of his book are devoted to other aspects of reincarnation. In the chapter 'Phoenix from the Ashes', he not only describes martyred souls reincarnated into Judaism bringing with them old wisdom and new impulses. This applies equally to Native Americans who met in Denver in 1987 in a 'cosmic Convergence' and also accept reincarnation as a fact.

Gershom pleads for a rainbow society in which each karmic group can find its place. He also feels that the dualistic aspect of the age of Pisces should give way to global unity in diversity in an Aquarian age. As a Rabbi he is very group minded and sees the working of reincarnation strongly from the angle of belonging to a group over many incarnations.

—ɷ—

The following text examplifies the working of destiny in how the book came about: (from chapter one of 'Beyond the Ashes')

"In March 1986 I completed my rabbinical thesis and was finally ordained by Rabbi Schachter-Shalomi. Now at last I had time to begin writing about my reincarnation findings. But once again I met with resistance. No Jewish publication would touch it, while publications on alternative spirituality still did not want to deal with the Holocaust. It seemed that reincarnation was a fine topic if you were discussing events that happened thousands of years ago. Everybody enjoyed to be told that he or she might have been an Egyptian princess or a Tibetan monk, but the possibility of having died recently in a concentration camp was just too horrifying. And, quite frankly, some of the editors I contacted felt that combining the Holocaust with reincarnation would offend the Jewish community. – Then in November, 1986, Venture Inward magazine, published by the Association for Research and Enlightenment, Inc. (A.R.E.), ran an article on Jews who were studying the teachings of Edgar Cayce, a well-documented American psychic known as the "sleeping prophet." The article was entitled "The Dilemma of Christ-Oriented Readings" and dealt with the difficulties many Jews had experienced in studying the Cayce material because of his heavily Christian orientation. Nevertheless, in spite of this theological "language barrier," the Jewish members of A.R.E. had persevered in their studies because, they believed, the teachings of Cayce had universal applications that went beyond religious differences. In his own lifetime, Edgar Cayce's clairvoyance had been considered an amazing phenomenon. Although he had no medical training whatsoever, while in deep trance, he could correctly diagnose patients "at a distance" merely by knowing the person's name and location at the time of the consultation. Time after time he was proven correct, often effective. Although Cayce was repeatedly investigated by skeptics during the forty-three years that he demonstrated this ability, no indications of fraud were ever found. – When Cayce died in 1945, he left behind him over 14,000 stenographic records of clairvoyant consultations that he had given for over 6,000 different people. These "Readings", as they are called, are preserved at the A.R.E. Headquarters in Virginia Beach, Virginia, and are still studied today by both medical doctors and laypersons. In addition to diagnoses, many of the readings contain information about spiritual growth of the clients. One of the central ideas in them is that, in almost every case, the person who received the reading had lived on earth many times before and that events in past lives were often affecting this life, both in the form of physical disease and in problems of daily living. In other words, Edgar Cayce taught reincarnation. – The above-mentioned Venture Inward article had caught my eye because here was a publication produced by a reputable organisation that was at least willing to discuss Jewish issues in the context of metaphysical studies. Could this be a place to publish my findings on reincarnation and the Holocaust? – I sent a query to editor A. Robert Smith and yes he would definitely be interested. The article was somewhat long for their format, bur Smith was so impressed with the case histories that he willingly gave me the space. Thus it was that Venture Inward officially broke the story when "Are Holocaust Victims Returning?" appeared in the November/December 1987 issue. – Neither Smith nor I was prepared for the enormous response. Within a week of publication, the Venture Inward office began receiving replies from readers, which they forwarded to me. Many of the letters were from people who had been deeply touched by the article because they felt that they, too, had been reincarnated after the Holocaust. And they gave fascinating details which further confirmed what I had already found. Some even sent tapes of their regression under hypnosis."

Reported in "Take a Break" Magazine, February 2011

A little boy of 3 ½ was suddenly diagnosed with leukemia. His mother was with him for initial tests, staying in hospital. He told her that she had a little girl in her tummy, called "India". The mother found out a few weeks later that she was indeed pregnant. Throughout his treatment he often asked: "Is India coming today?" He would talk to his mother about India coming and his mother used these converstions to keep his spirits up during hard days. "What would you like to do when India comes"? "Where shall we take her" etc. The little boy would often lay his head on his mother's growing bump and sing "You are my sunshine...". Near the end of his treatment India arrived!! The little boy gazed in wonder at his little sister and started to sing (very quietly "You are my sunshine"... At that moment the mother describes how she saw her son and daughter full of light – "Like an Angel" and felt (for the first time since the little boy got sick) total peace and the belief that all would be well.

Karin T-U – How a toddler
surprised his mother

Karin T-U. How a Toddler surprised his mother
Told to the author by his mother.

"My four year old son was playing with toys
on the floor, when he suddenly looked up to me and
said: "Mummy, you have a baby in your tummy". I
was utterly surprised because neither I, nor anybody
knew anything about it. "Are you sure?" I asked, and
he confirmed that it was so. "Is it a boy or a girl?" I
enquired. And he replied: "She is a girl, she comes
from China and her name is Chang". He then turned
to his toys and that was the end of this entirely unexpected conversation.

When the baby was born – a girl – the brother
welcomed her overjoyed, as a very old friend: "There
she is, there she is"!

The boy developed a keen interest in eastern
religions and martial arts during his teenage years,
and said several times that he felt a very special connection to his little sister."

Chapter 4

Consciousness outside the body and contacts to and from beyond

During each of the two World Wars quite extraordinary events of consciousness outside the body and contacts to and from beyond were experienced and documented, both of which also shed a bright light on the period between incarnations.

In 1915, a young German artist, Sigwart, met his death after being fatally wounded. He succeeded after his death to communicate with his sister, also a musician, involving his whole family and a circle of friends. In the early stages the communications were very frequent, later more intermittent. They continued until 1944 and a selection was published in 1970 under the title 'Bruecke ueber den Strom' (Bridge over the Stream).

(Translation: JMS)

The second was a 20 year old US Private in military training who contracted pneumonia in dusty conditions in Texas and clinically died in the Army hospital at Camp Barkeley in 1943. He was miraculously revived after nine minutes. Later, an MD and Psychiatrist, George G Ritchie, told his amazing story in 'Return from Tomorrow'. Dr Raymond A Moody, author of 'Life after Life', listened as a student to Ritchie's story in 1965 which sowed the seed to his own later research.

Both events are of profound significance, not only in regard to 'thinking without the brain' or consciousness beyond death. Both of them, in very different ways, give insights into the nature of the interim period between incarnations, called by Rudolf Steiner – the 'spiritual world'.

At the risk of doing injustice to both these unique events – which should be studied in their full context – I take it upon my conscience to present here some quotations of the first and a digest of the second, because the impact of this knowledge can become a turning point for our understanding and appreciation of the interim period as the 'workshop' of working out our karma.

After his fatal injury, Sigwart still had a few weeks in hospital before his death. He was a promising composer and had volunteered for the army at the outbreak of war. As he was later able to communicate, he was given special permission, due to a karmic precondition, to do so, and it was very hard for him to find 'an open ear', to his thought transmission. Once established and recognised as being genuine, the revelations, guidance and encouragements became ever more insightful and subtle, based on love and true devotion. The first two communications are given in full:

Sigwart – Bridge over the Stream

Sigwart an artist soldier who died in the war, contacting his sister

28th July 1915: "I myself, am speaking, I, your brother Sigwart, who loves you, who is around you and so closely entwined with you all. You may no longer mourn, that is so frustrating to me. Make yourself free from all thoughts of sorrow. You have always been my brothers and sisters which we will be always. I see you have now grasped everything aright; now nothing can separate us. Tell it to my siblings, tell it [also] to my/our parents, whom I thank for everything. You have to become the mediator; after long struggles I have succeeded to communicate. Already at the beginning I wanted to but you did not respond. Through your great love and sensibility I can draw closer. You will be glad because through me you will advance and learn very much, because I died also for you in order to communicate the teachings of the spirit."

29th July: "Now I am pleased with you. Initially your grief was a burden for me. I then made the greatest effort to make myself noticeable [to your feelings]. Now it is better. How easy it is to die! I am not yet allowed to tell you everything. All is very, very well with me and you should think of me as a figure of light, who has no longer to carry any pain. I have caused my death myself, because I was meant to engage in some greater task here. Of these works you have no idea, you can hardly imagine how beautiful, how great, how perfect they are. Hail the one, who is allowed to accomplish them! Your body seeks rest. Sleep, as much as you can. In sleep we meet and help each other. Soon you will know it also in waking. this is the first beginning. If you only knew how much of beauty I have experienced here already! I shall once show it to you myself. Inevitable laws are around you to live your life as you have caused it yourself."

These first two communications make it clear how individual these communications are. In the case of Sigwart we are allowed to meet a highly developed individuality. Of general importance is the knowledge that the continued grieving and sorrowing are of hindrance to making contact and receiving communications either in sleeping or in the waking state. On 30th of July he says: "Don't think that now, as a spiritual brother, I could experience less joy together with you than formerly as a human being. I have not changed, except, I don't carry any more a physical body. I know much more now and feel happy to be allowed to fulfil a great mission. But otherwise I have remained as the one you knew. Everything is so much purer and clearer. That I should see it like this already in this early stage I had not expected. Thanks to my interest in the supersensible, I did not experience disappointments; to the contrary: It was an awakening more beautiful than you can imagine. Everything impressed itself on me and I was immediately aware what had happened to me, – namely that I had passed the 'threshold of death', as you call it rightly."

From communication of 2nd August: "What is the use of acquired knowledge if the human being does not know what happens with him after death! — Now, I would, if still on earth, rather forgo all earthly knowledge if it would [otherwise] mean losing the faith in the future after death! This is the basic thought and everything else , by comparison, is nothing." From 6th August: "The battles in the spiritual world are far more intensive than war on earth, because here the issue is the annihilation of the spirit (the individuality); in your wars, the body is being destroyed. ... For how long I shall remain on this present spiritual level,

I do not know; I believe, however, not long any more. Then I shall rise from my present body, similarly to when you leave behind your physical body." S. tells his sister how close he is to her when she plays music; he is right in the music. … Don't think that I guide your hand, I [only] touch your hand but do not push. I speak the sentence you should write down. This is the process of my transmission. Now I have other work waiting. God be with you!"

9th August: Sigwart speaks about the strength-giving quality of the sun also in yonder realm. He refers to the quality and effects of the planets and says: "…All this is so unspeakably deep and great that one cannot but be amazed. How I regret that I have not yet gained a clearer image of it. The human brain can hardly grasp the vastness of these things which surround us and the earth. Daily my will to know grows stronger and daily I gain more insight. … Of our acquaintances I have met no one yet. I also think it will be hard to find someone, because with none of the deceased a true bond has been forged. Only those who truly love one another will find together! The space in which we are is so vast that it is impossible to meet by chance. How small your earth is by comparison." 27th September: …Every truly high-minded thought which has its origin in the Godhead draws man in time out of his bodily sheaths and gives him the strength and the wish to free himself. By the strings of his own thoughts the human soul is uplifted and drawn upward. Therefore the thoughts are of the highest importance and not the deeds. The thoughts play a greater part, everything one can reach with them, with deeds, however, only little. Take note of this, then you can progress so much easier. Now you have opened the doors. The more your faith grows strong, the closer we are to each other. However, a lot you have to learn still, but never be discouraged. You have to reach the goal and will achieve what you have been called for to do."

So much as an introduction to the revelations, encouragements and guidance, sometimes in the form of verses, meditations and prayers given to those closest to him. The first volume covers 1915, the second 1916, the third to 1919 and the last to 1944, including some messages by the sister, who died in 1935. One thing has become very clear: The interval between incarnations is filled with higher consciousness and what we have learned so far, disproves the notion of a vacant waiting time for souls to await the last trumpet, nor that this is merely a 'rest in peace'. Whatever height and distance from the earth is achieved, the relationship to the earth is never lost. In conclusion of this introduction part of a description of an Easter celebration shall leave an impression of the grandeur of experience:

"I am here, Sigwart. So listen: We, too, have an Easter celebration, however, it is something quite different that we celebrate [here].You celebrate the reappearance, the resurrection of Christ Jesus, with us it is the reunion with the higher parts of His being which He has left behind during His sojourn on earth. There is such a nameless and deep self-overcoming by Christ in this separation which He had taken upon Himself that one can only kneel before the greatness of His deed. All of us here have only been able to sense what the descent of such a high being as the Christ, truly signifies. In spite of my great reverence for this being of light whilst on earth, I was not even in the slightest way able to fathom who the Christ was. How this godly Being was able to taste all earthly misery, passing by nothing without deeply entering into it. This is greater than great; it is unfathomable and singular in the whole earth and world evolution."

Dr George G. Ritchie –
Return from Tomorrow

George G Ritchie, a soldier who was revived from clinical death

The story of George Ritchie is of great significance, told in his book 'Return from Tomorrow, being the first account of clinical death and out-of body experiences. The student Raymond Moody was one of the listeners to one of the first lectures Ritchie gave on this subject. Althoughat the time he was not yet ready to engage in it, it gave him the impulse to his later research and publication of his seminal book 'Life After Life' of which over 75 million copies have been sold. Moody dedicated his work to Ritchie with the enigmatic words:" To George Ritchie, MD, and through him , to the One whom he suggested" The answer to this riddle is found in the following excerpts from Return from Tomorrow.

The US Private George G Ritchie, having caught pneumonia at Camp Barkley's, Texas, during training, was admitted to the military hospital. He had been invited for the entrance examination to the medical school at Richmond and hoped he would be well enough in time to travel. After some improvement he suddenly collapsed and went into intensive care. That night, the ward boy found him without a sign of life and reported. The Officer on Duty pronounced him dead and gave orders for the body to be moved to the morgue. The sheet was pulled over his head. The compelling wish to attend the examination gave force to the soul to leave the body and to move at great speed in the direction to distant Richmond. All along his mind was registering the changing landscape, arguing with himself whether he moved in the right direction. When reaching a town, he landed himself on a pavement and wanted to ask direction from a pedestrian. He seemed neither to see, nor to hear him, and, planting himself in front of him, the fellow walked right through him. He realised that the same thing had happened in the hospital and concluded he should return. With the speed of light he was back but found it hard to identify the right block and ward and his bed. Drawn towards his body, he saw a shrouded lump and only recognised his ring on a hand that stuck out from under the sheet. Whilst he pondered the situation, the light increased. How could the 15 watt bedside lamps be so bright? The light became too bright to look at. "...now I saw that it was not light but a Man who had entered the room, or rather, a Man made out of light, though this seemed no more possible to my mind than the incredible intensity of the brightness that made up this form. The instant I perceived Him, a command formed itself in my mind. 'Stand up!' The words came from inside me, yet they had an authority my mere thoughts had never had. I got to my feet, and as I did came the stupendous certainty: 'you are in the presence of the Son of God' – Again the concept seemed to form itself inside me, but not as thought or speculation. It was a kind of knowing, immediate and complete... Above all, with the same mysterious inner certainty, I knew that this man loved me. Far more even than power, what emanated from this Presence was unconditional love... When I say that He knew everything about me, this was simply an observable fact...".

Ritchie then describes his coming to terms with this experience. He was obliged to confront his whole past in the same speed and realised all his pride and had to answer to the question that came from the Presence close to him: "What did you do with your life?" All the time he had to see, situations where pride inflated him and how little he had cared for others and given little thought to the stories he heard of Jesus Christ. In himself he heard the voice saying: "I told you so!" "Still wanting to justify myself, how could He have told me and I not heard? I told you by the life I lived. I told you by the death I died. And if you keep your eyes on Me, you will see more ... With a start I noticed we were moving. I hadn't been aware of leaving the hospital, but now it was nowhere in sight. The living events of my life which had crowded around us had vanished too; instead we seemed to be high above the earth, speeding together towards a distant pin-prick of light. It wasn't like the out-of-body travel I experienced earlier. Then my own thoughts obsessed me... [but now] my eyes on Him, as He commanded, this mode of movement no longer seemed strange or alarming."

With his eyes on his guide, their speed-journey takes them to a distant harbour town. He sees shades following human beings, forever expressing their regret. "What are these and why do they always say "I am sorry" and no one hears it? The answer came again from within: "They have taken their own life". With his guide, they enter what seemed a sailors' pub. There the disembodied people mixed with the sailors. Some, with their non-physical hands tried to snatch cigarettes from smokers, others tried for the glasses of liqueur. "The 'I' noticed a striking thing. A number of men standing at the bar seemed unable to lift their drinks to their lips. Over and over I watched them clutch at their shot glasses, hands passing through the solid tumblers, through the heavy wooden counter top, through the very arms and bodies of the drinkers around them. And these men, every one of them, lacked the aureole of light that surrounded the others." It was the stuff of nightmares, experienced and told in great detail. But worse experiences were to follow: "Which ever way I looked, He remained the real focus of my attention. Whatever else I saw, nothing compared to Him… Now, however, we were apparently still somewhere on the surface of the earth, I could see no living man or woman. The plain was crowded, even jammed with hordes of ghostly discarnate beings, nowhere was there a solid, light-surrounded person to be seen. All of these thousands of people were apparently no more substantial than I myself. And they were the most frustrated, the angriest, the most completely miserable beings I had ever laid eyes on. "Lord Jesus!" I cried. "Where are we?" At first I thought we were looking at some great battle-field: everywhere people were locked in what looked like fights to death, writhing, punching, gouging. It couldn't be a present-day war because there were no tanks or guns. No weapons of any sort, I saw as I looked closer, only bare hands and feet and teeth. And then I noticed that no one was apparently injured. There was no blood, no bodies on the ground; a blow that ought to have eliminated an opponent would leave him exactly as before." The gruesome images and searching thoughts, trying to find an explanation, seemed to carry on still for a long time. And Ritchie reflects "Perhaps it was not Jesus who had abandoned them, but they who had fled from the Light that showed up their darkness. ... Almost from the beginning I had sensed it ... That entire plain was hovered over by beings seemingly made of light. It was their very size and blinding brightness that had prevented me at first from seeing them. Now that I had adjusted my eyes... I could see that these immense presences were bending over the little creatures on the plain, perhaps even conversing with them. Were these bright beings angels? Many questions arose in George Ritchie's soul. "And suddenly I realised that there was a common denominator to all these scenes so far. It was the failure to see Jesus. Whether it was a physical appetite, an earthly concern, an absorption with self – whatever got in the way of His Light created the separation into which we stepped at death."

The next chapter adds another dimension to Ritchie's experience. On the move again, they approached a realm that appeared like a university. "Again, it was as if Jesus could reveal only as much as my mind could grasp." He wanted to compare his sights to something familiar. "Except that to compare what I was now seeing with anything on earth was ridiculous. It was more as if all the schools and colleges in the world were only piecemeal reproductions of

151

this reality." He met very serious learning situations: a phantastic library, musical achievements of the highest order. Everything seemed to emanate from a high source of inspiration." Is this ...heaven, Lord Jesus?" I ventured. The calm, the brightness, they were surely heaven-like! So was the absence of self, or clamouring ego. "When these people were on earth, did they grow beyond selfish desires?" "They grew, and they have kept growing." The answer shone like sunlight in that intent and eager atmosphere." "The central fact, the all-adequate one, remained this personality at my side. Whatever additional facts he was showing me, He remained the real focus of my attention." George Ritchie had still glimpses of yet higher planes and a premonition of the Heavenly Jerusalem, but then: "He had shown me all He could; now we were speeding far away. Walls closed around us ... it was several seconds before I recognised the little hospital room we had left what seemed a lifetime ago. Jesus still stood beside me, otherwise consciousness could not have sustained the transition from infinite space to the dimensions of this cell-like room. ... But incredibly Jesus was telling me that I belonged somehow with that sheeted form, that His purpose for me involved that lump-like thing as well." He cried out in desperation that Jesus should not leave him.

According to hospital records approximately nine minutes had passed since Private Ritchie was pronounced dead. Now the ward boy returned to get the body ready for transfer to the morgue. But surely that hand on the blanket had moved? Galloping he went to the O.D., who came, examined him once more and pronounced him dead. "Doubtless the young orderly on the long, lonely night shift, was imagining things. And then occurred the event the full impact of which only registered with me years later. At the time I learned of it I was surprised certainly, but not dumfounded as I am today each time I think of it. The ward boy refused to accept the verdict of his superior officer. "Maybe, you could give him a shot of adrenalin directly into the heart muscle." It was unthinkable for a private to argue with an officer, especially on a medical matter. But it was done and a lengthy road to recovery had begun.

This was not the only time that Ritchie's life was saved. Posted in France after D-Day, another miraculous event took place. The telling of his story only occurred slowly. Very few people were able to open their heart without doubting. But Ritchie experienced the same Presence in his listeners as the one that was leading him on this singular journey.

George Ritchie's fascinating story is reminding one of Charles Dickens 'Christmas Carol'. Yet it is not the product of poetic imagination. When Ritchie, many years later, as a medical doctor and psychiatrist applied for a position at the University of Virginia, he was interviewed by a top professor in the Department of Psychiatry and the remark was put to him as a question: "Well, Dr Ritchie, I understand that you feel that you have met the Christ." Ritchie continues: "I saw my chances at the University of Virginia floating out of the window. Dr Abse was a Jew, a Freudian analyst, and he was asking me a discrete question which demanded an answer. Under my breath, as I had done so often, I turned to Jesus: 'Lord, what do I say now?' 'Deny me before man,' – 'the words seemed almost audible, 'and I will deny you before my Father.'

To Dr Abse I said: I can no more deny the reality of what happened to me at Barkeley, Texas, than Saul of Tarsus could deny what happened to him on the road to Damascus." Had Ritchie tried to hide his experience, he would have been dismissed as unreliable. He was given the position and became good friends with the professor.

These last two entirely different stories agree in substance, although they are from different continents, from different nationalities and cultural backgrounds, and different historical periods. The common denominators are the two World Wars with waves of deaths on unparalleled proportions.

Dr Raymond A. Moody – Life After Life

Raymond A Moody, a physician, author of Life after Life

The new revised edition of 'Life After Life', which first appeared in 1975, is introduced with a Preface by his former student, Melvin Morse, MD and a Foreword by Elisabeth Kübler-Ross, MD. As mentioned above, the book, a bestseller, fell on fertile ground. It has opened the minds and hearts of multi-millions of contemporaries to the consciousness of near-death experiences.

The question of consciousness independent of the human brain, is still an unsolved scientific problem as the sentences from the Preface suggest:" He (Moody) inspired me to think critically about the experiences and their implication for understanding the nature of human consciousness. The fact that dying comatose brains can be conscious and aware of their surroundings, as well as interact with another spiritual reality (another brain?), has profound implications for our understanding of how the brain works.

Raymond Moody continues with his research, teaches and has written several other books and has built his own 'Theater of the Mind', as he calls his modern psychomanteum. "Why should we wait until we die to have this remarkable transformative experience?" he asks. The Preface states: "Raymond Moody's Life After Life reconnects us with a timeless wisdom about death. We do not simply die; death is far more complicated than that. We die conscious, with an expanded awareness of this reality coupled with a greater understanding of our lives. ..."

The Development of Consciousness

Rodolf Steiner's concept of history is primarily that of a development of consciousness. In his Spiritual Science he describes our own historical period as the 'Age of the consciousness-soul' which started with the advent of natural science in the fifteenth century. The preceeding period, dominated by Greece and Rome, he called the 'mind-soul' period. Still earlier, the time of ancient Egypt, Assyria and Babylon, is called the 'sentient-soul' period. Steiner rejected the common trend of projecting present-day mentality on the way of thinking and feeling of earlier ages.

In the development of consciousness in our age,

what are the recogniseable stages? It started with an enhanced awareness of the physical-material world that lead to the gradual development of natural science, no longer trusting in the traditional authorities but relying on the experiment. This produced an entirely new way of thinking which followed the laws of the mineral world and explained the world with mechanical arguments in space, time and energy. The essence of life, soul and spirit became elusive. Every concept had to be based on hard evidence and facts that could be weighed and measured. In tandem with this dominent male dominated awareness of an outer world there run a more female stream aware of the neglected aspects of life, soul and spirit which found an expression in poets, artists and philosophers. A future age started to shed its light on the hidden side of life. The onesidedness and excesses of the mainstream began to be questioned and challend. What does it mean to be human and individual? The suffragettes pioneered the equality for women; the unprecedented destruction of the environmentr ushered in the environmental and ecological movement; the alarming extinction of animal and plant spieces brought about the creation of national parks and the re-introduction of spieces locally extinct. In each of these cases of heighted awareness it depended in the first place on individuals who had the courage to speak out and challenge the status quo. They were branded as heretics, dissidents, revolutionaries or considered insane because they dared to challenge previlege, profit and power. The idea that every human being is a species in him/herself which underlies the truth of reincarnation is met, therefore, with great resistence. The acceptance of this truth could herald a sea-change beneficial to the individual and society. Raymond Moody and Elisabeth Kuebler-Ross have extended their quest to the process of dying and gained insights into experiences after death. There remained, however, still one great gulf to bridge: the acceptance of a consciousness entirely free of the body. A courageous leap from natural science to spiritual science is required! Then no reference to a comatose brain is required in order to accept that the soul has not only a vision of the life just ended, but has even a preview – before conception – of the life to come. Without this extention of consciousness no knowledge can be gained of the period between incarnations, described in much detail by spiritual science. This does not mean that everything is pre-ordained. A higher part of the self was involved in preparing, or choosing the events to come but the present self can respond creatively, engaging free will through insight. The knowledge that higher powers are involved in human life is demonstrated by many accounts presented in this book.

Chapter 5

Contacts to and from Beyond

In the following, some exceptional phenomena are presented, which will show several significant links to the world of spirit. It is more realistic to acknowledge such a spirit world in its own rights, rather than only as a kind of waiting room between incarnations. (Rudolf Steiner even describes three worlds of spirit.) Three examples will be given of direct, sincere and genuine communication with beings dwelling in the spirit world. The first are 'letters' dictated to Lord Dowding, sent by soldiers who died in combat; the second is by means of direct voice – Douglas Conacher: the third is by thought transference or telepathy – Bob Woodward. Lastly a reference is made to an important book.

Lord Dowding – Letters from Men Killed in the War.

These letters are contained in his book 'Many Mansions' (1973) and are found on the web, and reprinted here. Considering the ongoing casualties in continued conflict, it is astonishing that they are not more widely known and referred to. They could be of great help and comfort to many families and friends.

The veracity and genuine nature of these

documents are vouchsaved by the individual style in which they are written and the man who received and published them is Lord Dowding, the famous Air Chief Marshal of the Battle of Britain. His Father, alive on yonder side, acted as the guide to those men, encouraging them to turn to Lord Dowding who had the gift of receiving these messages.

Great insights may be gleaned from these 'Letters'. Not only do they agree with the certainty of life and consciousness after death, they also affirm the existence and active involvement of guides in various guises – according to the respective state of comprehension of each individual. They furthermore confirm and reveal their inner life – of soul and spirit – and point to the existence of a many layered spirit world.

The Letters describe the experiences of those who have just died and how they are helped to come to terms with their new form of life and their moving on to higher planes of the spirit world.

From a sailor, the son of an old friend.

I was in an oil tanker and we were all drowned when she was hit. It was very quick and I did not suffer any pain but tremendous surprise at finding myself possessed of the most wonderful strength and able to heave away all kinds of wreckage. I was making my way through the debris when I realised that we were moving through deep water. It was so still that it was just like a dream. I remember that it was quite easy to move and there was no difficulty in breathing (if we were breathing), but now I come to think of it, it was a different sort of breath. Anyhow I got free and so did some of my friends and we moved away without quite knowing what we were doing. We found a stranger had joined us, his clothes were quite dry and he walked through the water without it seeming to touch him. I noticed this and after a time I said something to him about it.

It all seemed so queer, and as we walked I saw that we were going towards what looked like a sunrise, the best I have ever seen, and I turned to look back over the way we had come, and the stranger put his hand on my shoulder and said "Not yet, you must go on out of the Valley of the Shadow of Death and then you can return if you want to". I said "Oh, I don't care" and I went on in a dazed sort of way until we came to a kind of garden, but it wasn't enclosed. It was on the hillside with lots and lots of flowers; oh, they were lovely! By this time I had realised that we were not walking in the water any more and I felt so tired and sleepy, and my feet refused to go any further. The stranger suggested that we should rest so I sat down on the grass and was soon asleep.

You cannot imagine my astonishment on waking to find myself in a strange place, and I couldn't first remember how I got there; but it came back after a time, and I found some of the others and they let me piece it together with their help. But all the time the stranger stayed with us, and he listened and said nothing, so at last I asked him where he come from, and why he had brought us here, and he said: "Oh, I'm just a seaman like you, but I've been on shore for some time now so I thought I might be able to help you. Then, very slowly, we all knew that we were what we used to call "dead," but it was so different that I couldn't believe it.

It's grand, just GRAND! I wish my Mother could know about it. We were in a far better land than the one we left, and it's all O.K. I'd love her to see it. Dad came to me soon after I realised this and we had a great time together. It seems queer to call him Dad, he's younger than I am now, at least he looks it. We are to have a job together soon, but I am not to be in a hurry.

From a New Zealander.

Can I try? (to write) I do not find it difficult but what is the use of trying? You do not know my people, they are far away and would never understand. I am one of the Colonial troops and my name is Simson. I came from New Zealand. I guess some of the lads had their fill of fighting, but that was what we came for, and I am glad I came. I know it wasn't much use in the ordinary way, but we showed our loyalty to Britain, and that's the spirit that will prevail in the end. I was one of the casualties in Greece. I feel I should go home now, but I can't leave my mates. I could go as swiftly as thought, and return equally quickly, but time doesn't matter now and if that's so, let's go doing it.

I am rather vague as to who is "alive" and who is "dead", they all look much alike. But my parents would never understand, so it's no use trying to tell them. I am going straight on with my job, under my own officer, and with many of my pals, we work for the rest, especially when they are asleep. Sometimes we raid the enemies "dead" battalion, fighting with our thought weapons! It's a grand game. There are so few things we can't do now. One of the strangest things is that we all feel happy. I wasn't one of the naturally happy ones on Earth. I worried and fidgeted and found time lagged more than most people. But here there is a sort of care-free feeling, and no time to lag, so I can't work up any regret over leaving my body. I stay right here. Our boys are happy , too, all of them, and the others are having such a hard time that it is up to us to stay by them.

Question. "Can we help you? Do you need our help?"

Well, yes, we do. It's ever such a help to do this, it kind of gives me more pep to get into close touch with my pals. I would be much better if you could have a talk with more of us… You give us confidence. So often we cannot see the result of our work, but now I can see and feel your reactions, and it makes real work, like I expect it does for you. Something to show for it. Thank you ever so much. I think that's all for now. Good night.

Gunner Simson.

From a Norwegian.

Thank you, I feel rather strange doing this, but it goes quite easy. I am Not English, nor even British, I am Norwegian. I have lived in England for many years and I find your language as easy as mine own.

I was shot by the Germans at Trondheim. I was a little shopkeeper; they shoot. I do not love the Germans. I never shall, but I am held up here by my hatred. I find that I cannot throw it off. I still feel so angry for their acts of unprovoked cruelty., and I am consumed with my passionate anger, and cannot get free. I beg of you to help me. Your Father, he bring me to you to make a close link with him. He tell me that we must forgive the Nazis, and they do not know what they do; that they are like sleep-walkers, and until I forgive them I cannot get free to pass from this plane so near the Earth on to other planes.

Here all that happens with you is known and felt in a greater form and we go on feeling more and more animiosity against the German race, and when they join us in the astral body we feel far more antagonism than we felt during our Earth-life. It is awful, this anger that we cannot shake it off. Give me serenity and let me sleep. I want to sleep and forget them. I might be fairer in my judgement and come to forgive.

I see why Christ quickly forgave everyone before He left the Earth Body. I see the reason and the need, and with the help of your Father and the contact that you have given me, I shall escape.

J. Ammussen.

A Highlander taken prisoner in Crete.

Yes, I was in Crete. I'm a Highlander. I was in the Marines and stayed in Crete among those who couldn't be taken off. It was one of the worst moments when I saw the ships and know it was hopeless for us to hope for any escape. I got hit in the shoulder, and there was nothing for it but to give in and let them take me prisoner. I was put on a stretcher and taken to hospital, but they did nothing for me exept to give me a bed to lie on, and my wound got septic and very painful. I got delirious. I suppose, and they questioned me, but I don't think they did anything for me, perhaps they couldn't. I don't know. Anyway, after ages and ages of suffering I seemed to pass into a timeless sleep, and when I woke up there was no pain and I was out of doors so I thought I had escaped and I wandered about glad to be free, but I couldn't make sense of it all. I seemed unable to walk properly, I couldnt keep on the ground, and though I didn't fall it was extremely difficult to move along, and then the whole place would grow misty. I would see places and people one moment and the next I saw something quite different. I thought I was delirious again. Now I know that I was seeng two planes at once, and I hadn't learned to manage my spirit body; it worried me a lot and I got quite hopeless. People would come up to help me, and just as we were beginning to understand each other I would see the outline of Crete, and be overcome with the desire to hide away from the Germans. It was a sort of torture, and when at last they got through to me and I was able to sleep – the real sleep of death – the putting off of one life and the taking on of another. I don't know much about it, but this life seems so natural that I was anxious to try to write through you so as to test my power on the physical plane before going back to help those who have suffered as I did. I know we can and I don't want to waste time. It's grand finding that nothing has been wasted. I have all the faculties now that I longed to have on Earth. Oh, it's simply grand…

Goodnight.

Two letters from a Polish pilot who spent his last leave with us.

Yes, I am shot down and out. I have survived many flights but not this one. I am wounded, I cannot control the aircraft. It was my leg, you feel the pain, I could not move the controls and fall, I cannot leave the aircraft, I fall quite consciously. I get up without any pain, I see my observer and gunner, he is hurt too but not so much. The Germans come to find us, they do not see me, I run and hide, but they not look for me. My friend they take away. I wander about. I feel well and cannot think how I crashed the aircraft. My leg is healed. I wander about. I go to the French peasants and ask for help but they do not see me and I begin to wonder. I am neither hungry nor thirsty, nor particularly tired. I begin to see things changing. I see colours everywhere; it is sunset or sunrise and it looks as if the colours were reflected in the earth as well as in the sky. I lay and watched the colours take form; it was like a cinema when one picture fades out and another takes its place. I was astounded. I do not know where I am. I ask, I pray, I forget that I have no faith in religion, I pray for help and it comes to me. Someone looking very strange , and yet quite like ourselves, come to me. He tells me not to mind the change; it is best for all and that I shall be happy in this land. I am very confused. I think I am taken prisoner, then he explains that there are no prisons or prisoners and I feel free again. He took me away and told me to sleep. He touched my eyes and I sleep at once. When I wake he is still there and I am on Earth again in the occupied territory with Germans all round. I have come back to my body. I find it difficult to leave it.

I see no colours, but my new friend is there too, and he talks to me, but I can't see him well. They are doing something to my body. I am miserable so my friend tells me to think very hard of some place outside the war so I think very hard of the last time I see family life with you at H—, I see you all quite easily, and I wake you and you feel me near and you talk to me. I ask you to let me stay and just sit quietly in your house far from the battle until I can go on, and you say "Yes," so I stay. Now I begin to feel sleepy again. I am between the worlds. Help me to throw of this one and to go on – I want to go on – I think I can, please help me.

S.Z.

Several days later.

Thank you, yes I am well, I do not yet feel ready to leave your home for very long at a time, but I go for a short time, but it is food to come back to you all.

I am going now sometimes to Poland, but I dare not stay. I have no strength yet to help them and they need this power so badly. I see my old friends, some dying and some dead, but I can do nothing. I am tired, and feel too ill to reach them. We must help soon, but at present we are too weak.

Your Father, or someone like, he comes with me and we try to help but I am nearly useless; I want to help but I am like a child, I cannot. Also I never had faith, nothing to expect on dying and I am lost; I know nothing. All the things I made fun of come back to me, I was a bad man. I neglected many things, my prayers and my church, but I do not know if that mattered. I have no creed, and now I find that extinction being impossible, I have to suffer a kind of conscious extinction, knowing and feeling and yet being empty of strength.

What you expect here, that you find: you build your awakening, it is just as you imagined, at least that is what they told me. I expected nothing , so nothing came. But now I am pulling out of the difficult doldrums and am beginning to feel my strength. Thank you for helping.

S.Z

From a tank officer.

Thank You, I am alive after all. I thought that extinction was the only thing that could follow such an inferno. We seemed to go down on all sides, British and German alike, tanks, and guns and planes. I had the feeling that the machines of our own creation were exterminating us, they seemed so much stronger and more vindictive than the humans inside them. I believe it's the battle of the machines, they are in charge and we are the slaves of some evil genius through whom they have been created. I feel the influence of evil so strongly. I longed to get away and lie in the clean sand and forget the horrors of man's inferno of which we did not seem to be in charge.

I prayed for help when we stuck in the sand and fire broke out and prayed with all my soul and I know we couldn't escape, but prayer seemed to strengthen me and I felt that nothing really mattered so desperately, excepting the feeling of evil, and that had receded; I could not name it or explain in words. It seemed to meet us from the sand and hang all around the tank battle. I felt sick and miserable, and than it passed off and I found myself standing outside the tank talking to my colonel. He seemed unconscious of the bullets that were raining down on us. I ran for shelter but he called me and told me not to bother. He was looking as young as a subaltern and as though he was enjoying the battle. He took me by the shoulder and said "Don't you see, Kit, we are dead, and yet far more alive than they are, and we can go on fighting, hampering the enemy, throwing dust in their eyes, putting ideas into our leaders and playing an invisible hand.

Here are two people who would like to write. February 4th 1942.

Yes, I am very glad to have this chance, I always thought it might be so, but until I was picked off by a Jap sniper, I was never certain.

I fell face-downwards in the swampy jungle, and lay unconscious for some time in a sort of nightmare, my body was trying to reassert itself, and my spirit to get free. Never think that when people seem unconscious that they really are so, at least I wasn't. It was a time of conscious paralysis, I have it, and when something snapped and I was free I was awfully relieved.

I got back to our fellows and I soon realised what had happened when they did not see me; but I was so interested in finding myself unchanged that I hadn't time to think of anything else. I wanted to tell them not to fear death and all that. But I couldn't.

After a time I began to see the Jap dead, they were helping their own fellows, and the living Japs, and the living Japs could sometimes see and hear them, and they used all the information given, and this made me feel that we should be able to do the same. I tried awfully hard, but I couldn't warn or suggest anything which could be accepted by the brains of our fellows, so I wandered off wondering what to do next.

I did not exactly want to leave them to it, but there didn't seem to be any alternative, so I did. I wandered off into the forest, and for a time forgot all about the war, and all that my friends were going through because I was fascinated by the life that I saw all around me. The jungle is always rich in colour, sound and beauty of trees and flowers but now behind every thing that I knew so well lurked a hidden meaning, and some beautiful ray or sound seemed to permeate the very texture of the jungle life.

I can't explain. I was superbly happy, and entirely myself, but that self had grown in comprehension, and in power to experience contentment and bliss.

Then a voice came to my ears, and gradually I sensed a beautiful shining figure that said to me: "Here you see the land of pure content but you have left behind a land of passionate unrest. Do you not wish to help others to find the key to this place of joy?"

I was so overcome at never having thought of anyone else for ages that I must have blushed like a schoolboy, but the Shining One didn't seem to notice. So I stammered that I really hadn't grasped my whereabouts yet, and could he help me? He said: "No, you found the way, and the rest you must discover for yourself, but others may not be so fortunate and need helping."

I didn't want to turn my back on this glorious place, but the Shining One promised to come with me and not leave me. He explained that I could always return just by recalling this place vividly and wishing myself here, and now equally you and I must see ourselves in the battle zone.

I did so most regretfully, and anyway we seemed to pass, or rather there was no passing, one surrounding faded out and another took shape. The jungle moved or dissolved and it's place was taken by another sort of jungle full of men shouting orders and screaming in pain. I felt unable to bear it at first, but the Shining One said:" Come and stand by this man, he is about to pass over to our side." A second later and a bullet had ripped through his stomach and he lay groaning at our feet. The Shining One bent down and touched his head and eyes and instantly the groaning ceased and I saw his spirit leave his tortured body, and looking dazed and pale joined us in the deep foliage of the jungle. Before I know what had happened we were back in the wonderful jungle; It was a delicious experience.

The man who had joined us was one of our own men. A dull, quiet looking fellow. I hardly knew him. He took no interest in games and was always reading. Now he brightened up suddenly upon catching sight of me, and said: "Hellow, Sir, I didn't think you'd be here. I thought I'd seen you killed some days ago." I said: "yes, and I saw you killed some minutes ago."

The Shining One looked at me and I knew I shouldn't have broken the news so swiftly. But Burrows didn't seem to mind. "Oh, well, I've copped it, have I? Well, I don't care, it's awful fighting here and not much chance of getting out," was all he said. But What's it like here?" he continued.

I told him it was splendid, and that he had nothing to fear, and we walked about in the jungle clearing while the Shining One explained things to us. Soon we had both recovered from the shock and he took us back to the firing line to fetch more of our people and introduce them to this life. That is where we are now, and I wanted to get further and learn how to impress my thoughts upon the men in charge. I'm grateful to you for my first lesson; it doesn't seem to have gone too badly, but I'm tired now and I'll wish myself back in my jungle home of refreshment. I see there are no seperate places, all are moods within ourselves, just like what we were taught as children. "The Kingdom of God is within you." Good night.

A message from Libya.

O.K. I am glad, I've wanted to thank you for some time but couldn't make you hear.

We came abroad in the Spring. I was one of the Snodbury lot. I'll give you my name soon but you likely don't remember me. We was all split up and I was sent to Egypt. It was a show! I never thought as to how I could have lived through it. You know what I mean. I didn't think that dying was like this. I thought it was all over and finished; and sometimes we seemed to go through such a gruelling I didn't see how we could stand any more, and then, all of a sudden, it ceased and I was feeling upright as a trivet. A moment before I'd been dead beat and hot; oh, hot and thirsty with the most awful headache. The noise of battle fairly shattered me to bits, but then all of a sudden I was cool and fit and fresh as a daisy, and perky as could be, just looking on and hearing the noise, but not feeling shattered by it. I couldn't believe I was a "gonner." I saw my body just holed all over, and yet I couldn't believe it. I think I tried to pull it away from the gun, but there were others on top and beside me all in a heap. We'd got a direct hit all right.

The rest weren't there, that seemed queer to me, none of them, until I saw the officer. He come up to me and pointed to where his body lay. He gave a kind of gasp and said: "Oh, well, I suppose that's that. It's a queer world, Johnson, and I suppose we'd best carry on." I sais: "Yes Sir, but wot does we do now?" "Load the gun of course, you blighter," ses he, just as he used to. I went to obey, but strong as I felt I could not move the shells. They weren't so heavy as all that, but I could not get a hold of them; they was slippery. It seemed as though there was a sort of fish scale between my fingers and the shells. I couldn't hold it. I tells the officer and he comes to help, cursing proper he was by this time, and the two of us had a go, but would she budge? Not an inch. It seemed silly like; there was two great hefty fellows trying all we knew to lift one small ack-ack shell and we just couldn't do it. At last I broke down and laughed. "Well," I ses, "did you ever hear of two dead blokes firing a gun?" "Yes, I did," ses he all angry now and red in the face, "and wot's more, we are going to do it. We are fit enough, aren't we? Come on." So I heaved to again, thinking he'd gone crazy but that it was better to humour him. So we tried again, and now I begun to see things – not the efforts that we was making with our hands, if you follow me, but the Captain, he seemed to be sending out power some way, he was that determined, and I saw him, as you might imagine a Call Up Station of the wireless (if you could see one) and the answer came not through his fingers but through himself.

Lots of shadowy people came round us and worked with us, and the gun wasn't exactly in action, but something was being fired from her. Plane after plane came over, and suddenly lost speed then turned for home or crashed, I was mystified, I couldn't recollect anything like this: there seemed to be no noise, the discharge was silent, but the repercussion was distinctly felt by all of us, and that seemed to give us fresh impetus for the next. Just then I saw Jock coming towards us. He'd stopped a packet too, but he hadn't been with us before. He recognised me and the Captain and saluted and stood ready for duty. The Captain was too busy to notice him and Jock was always one for arguing, so I shut him up with "Just you wait and see, Son, we're learning new operational tactics, us three gonners from the old batch, so come along and learn and don't interrupt whatever you do." So I stayed close to Jock and made him watch the Captain. The Captain was a grand fellow, not a doubt. He seemed to drive his way through with all his determination against it all, and when I made a move, he looked up that sharp, and said: You sit quiet and think – for God's sake think with all the guts you've got in you, that's wot you must do now. We have got our brains and our determination and if we three hold together we'll pull it off and keep the air protection for our chaps. Can't you see the men who are helping us?" And then I looked and there was Sandy, who got sniped on Thursday, standing waist-high in water, making strange movements with his arms. I looked at his eyes, and they were Sandy's, but different, so clear like stars, he seemed inspired, if one could say so – .

I don't think I can finish the story today. May I stop now and come again? I've loved telling it to you. You see it's my first real adventure. Thank you.

Johnson.

Continuation

O.K. I'm all right. I'd like ever so much to finish what I was saying. Well, as I said Sandy looked inspired, I can't think of another word, and all at once he seemed to be leading us and not so much the officer who was following his orders most carefully, and as the shadow people became clearer I seemed to loose touch with the live people, and the dead ones seemed more real. Then the Jerries attacked and took the gun and we weren't touched. He came through us without seeing or hearing us, though we could see and hear him and feel the perspiry sense of his nearness. I loathed the smell all of a sudden, though it was familiar enough, it almost made me sick, and I saw Sandy and the Officer had moved away. So I pulled Jock up and said: "Don't let us lose sight of those two or we're lost. Jock agreed, but when I got to my feet I found I couldn't stand on the ground, it was most comical and so difficult to move on. I was kind of floating and so was Jock. I said: "Let's hold hands and keep each other down," but instead we

175

seemed to buoy each other up. Oh, we did have a time catching up with Sandy and the Captain, but they didn't notice us, someone else had joined them. He wasn't in uniform and I wondered for a minute how a civilian could have got there; he looked like an Arab, and then when he turned and looked at me, I felt – I felt as though he was re-making me all over again. I murmered "Christ" with all the reverence of a child. "No, not Christ, but a messenger from Him," said the man I was kneeling before, and "He wants you", that was what he said, He wanted me. "Whatever for?" I gasped out, and I looked up to see where the others were, but could see nothing but a blinding Light. It seemed to fill my head and burn through something that was keeping me there, and then a voice spoke again, something like this: "By your Sacrifice you have attained the Crown of Fortitude" – and then I remember no more.

That was the last I saw of Earth. I'd like some of the chaps to know how we pass on. It's a most wonderful thing.

I'm tired now and can't finish. Thank you.

Johnson.

ND! I wish my Mother could know about it. We were in a far better land than the one we left, and it's all O.K. I'd love her to see it. Dad came to me soon after I realised this and we had a great time together. It seems queer to call him Dad, he's younger than I am now, at least he looks it. We are to have a job together soon, but I am not to be in a hurry.

Two letters from a Polish pilot who spent his last leave with us.

Yes, I am shot down and out. I have survived many flights but not this one. I am wounded, I cannot control the aircraft. It was my leg, you feel the pain, I could not move the controls and fall, I cannot leave the aircraft, I fall quite consciously. I get up without any pain, I see my observer and gunner, he is hurt too but not so much. The Germans come to find us, they do not see me, I run and hide, but they not look for me. My friend they take away. I wander about. I feel well and cannot think how I crashed the aircraft. My leg is healed. I wander about. I go to the French peasants and ask for help but they do not see me and I begin to wonder. I am neither hungry nor thirsty, nor particularly tired. I begin to see things changing. I see colours everywhere; it is sunset or sunrise and it looks as if the colours were reflected in the earth as well as in the sky. I lay and watched the colours take form; it was like a cinema when one picture fades out and another takes its place. I was astounded. I do not know where I am. I ask, I pray, I forget that I have no faith in religion, I pray for help and it comes to me. Someone looking very strange , and yet quite like ourselves, come to me. He tells me not to mind the change; it is best for all and that I shall be happy in this land. I am very confused. I think I am taken prisoner, then he explains that there are no prisons or prisoners and I feel free again. He took me away and told me to sleep. He touched my eyes and I sleep at once. When I wake he is still there and I am on Easrth again in the occupied territory with Germans all round. I have come back to my body. I find it difficult to leave it.

I see no colours, but my new friend is there too, and he talks to me, but I can't see him well. They are doing something to my body. I am miserable so my friend tells me to think very hard of some place outside the war so I think very hard of the last time I see family life with you at H—, I see you all quite easily, and I wake you and you feel me near and you talk to me. I ask you to let me stay and just sit quietly in your house far from the battle until I can go on, and you say "Yes," so I stay. Now I begin to feel sleepy again. I am between the worlds. Help me to throw of this one and to go on – I want to go on – I think I can, please help me.

S.Z.

Several days later.

Thank you, yes I am well, I do not yet feel ready to leave your home for very long at a time, but I go for a short time, but it is food to come back to you all.

I am going now sometimes to Poland, but I dare not stay. I have no strength yet to help them and they need this power so badly. I see my old friends, some dying and some dead, but I can do nothing. I am tired, and feel too ill to reach them. We must help soon, but at present we are too weak.

Your Father, or someone like, he comes with me and we try to help but I am nearly useless; I want to help but I am like a child, I cannot. Also I never had faith, nothing to expect on dying and I am lost; I know nothing. All the things I made fun of come back to me, I was a bad man. I neglected many things, my prayers and my church, but I do not know if that mattered. I have no creed, and now I find that extinction being impossible, I have to suffer a kind of conscious extinction, knowing and feeling and yet being empty of strength.

What you expect here, that you find: you build your awakening, it is just as you imagined, at least that is what they told me. I expected nothing , so nothing came. But now I am pulling out of the difficult doldrums and am beginning to feel my strength. Thank you for helping.

S.Z

Douglas Conacher – A book dictated from Beyond

As this case is very exceptional. I will quote the flyer of the book published in 1973 under the title: CHAPTERS OF EXPERIENCE.

"Douglas Conacher has been 'dead' for nearly fifteen years, yet he is able to speak with his wife by independent voice communication. This remarkable book is a compilation of recordings made by Mrs Conacher during the sittings with the well-known medium Leslie Flint between 1965 and 1967.

In his twentieth-century life, Douglas Conacher was a deeply religious man, and ran a publishing firm in London, which produced books of an orthodox nature. Now, he has come to understand the true spirituality of man, and the reality of reincarnation. He gives us detailed and fascinating accounts of his previous lives, and speaks of how his quest for truth was a dominant factor in all of them. The variety of life experiences, which an individual soul may have had, is vividly revealed as he talks of priesthoods in the temples of Karnak and in Padua, of being a humble Jew at the time of Christ, of persecutions as a Hugenot and of a female incarnation during the French Revolution.

Douglas Conacher is a man who remains interested in the truth and, more importantly for those on earth, in disseminating of all that he has learned in the spirit-world; here he describes the life of the spirit-past, present and future – with earnestness and simplicity. In addition to a wealth of material ranging from living conditions and the role of the creative arts to communication by thought-forces and the abundance of love in the spirit-world, he presents us with a lucid explanation of the life-force and progression of the spirit of man.

Indisputably unusual because of its authorship, Douglas Conacher's work is even more valuable for its enlightening message; it is a book which puts us in touch with the potentialities of our own souls".

In her Introduction Mrs Eira Conacher sketches the background. Douglas died on 6th June 1958. They met 'by chance' when he, a confirmed bachelor was 58 and she, an arts teacher, was 39 years of age. He was a devout member of the Church of England and published orthodox religious and philosophical books. "Douglas was sensitive to beauty in all its manifestations but was not disposed to fanciful ideas". He was forthright and accuracy in all his statements was important to him. Reincarnation was not a matter dealt with mentally.

"In August 1959, I had the good fortune to meet Mr Leslie Flint – a well-known medium of integrity, who has the rare gift of independent direct voice mediumship – and to be invited to his evening circles. These were great occasions. Later, I had many private sittings with him. Douglas soon became a very good communicator by direct voice, and expressed the wish to concentrate on this form of communication.' He said: 'this is by far the most direct method, and the most satisfactory one, once one has become used to it. There is much less likelihood of the medium, or the recipient of the messages, influencing what is being given. This is as direct as one can ever hope to get. That is why I would like my books, preferably, to be what I have been able to give you in this manner."

—⁂—

"The medium, Mr Flint, does not go into trance, but remains normal throughout the séance, sometimes joining in the conversation'. 'The voices of the 'dead' do not emanate from his vocal organs. Usually, they seem to come somewhere between the medium and the sitter; occasionally, I have heard them come from high up in the room. These sittings with Mr Flint have always been absolutely natural and happy occasions."

—⁂—

I personally do not appreciate approaching the spirits of those who have died through seances. This book, however, struck me as exceptional and worth being included, also with respect to the message it contains.

Bob Woodward – Spirit Communications

The next paragraph is the story of a Camphill colleague of mine, Mr Bob Woodward. (Camphill communities are for people with special needs and were pioneered by Karl König, himself inspired by the work of Rudolf Steiner. Today these communities are to be found in many western countries). He has written a few books, one on Autism and one on Spirit Healing, and only later introduced me to another side of his activities: Spirit Communications. It was rather a surprise to me to learn of yet another of Bob's hidden talents. The caption on the cover tells the following: 'This is the story of one man's journey toward realising his full healing potential and ability'. First communicating with the spirit world through a medium, then learning to link directly, Bob Woodward shares with the reader his first recorded communications with his spirit teachers, who reassure him that they are working alongside him for the good of mankind and the fulfilment of God's grand plan.

Always questioning the validity and reality of these communications, Woodward confronts his own uncertainties about becoming a healer, as well as including his very personal communications with the spirits of his mother and father, in the hope that the reader can see 'how those who have died can indeed become the guides, helpers and counsellors of those on earth through a relationship grounded in love and freedom'.

Bob emphasised to me that it is his way to offer his thinking to the spirit in full clarity of consciousness. He sees the foundation of his relationship to the spirit most appropriately expressed in the words spoken by Jesus to the woman of Samaria (John, 4:23-25), 'But the time approaches, indeed it is already here, when those who are real worshippers will worship the Father in spirit and in truth. Such are the worshippers whom the Father wants. God is spirit, and those who worship him must worship him in spirit and in truth'

—∞—

In Conclusion of the book, Woodward writes:

"Even after having received many communications from Dr John and Joshua, I still wanted further confirmation that what I was receiving really stemmed from an independent source 'outside' me. To this end, I sent Anne (a befriended medium) a copy of one of the lengthy communications I had received from Joshua with the request that she 'check it out', so to speak: to ask Joshua if it really did come from him. I would now like to conclude this book with Joshua's words, as given to me by Anne in her ninth and last reading, dated 20 March 2006. Anne wrote: 'I sat this morning and asked Joshua for his input on what you had asked in your letter. Here are his words when you ask if it was him who spoke to you: 'He knows I did. When we communicate, the 'atmosphere', the 'presence' is different than when constructing one's own thoughts. He knows truly, inwardly, that it is I communicating, but he clearly does not want his own presence to be the dominant one. I have to use his brain, his electrons, his emotions, to give empathy and understanding (and) that is why it is complex to define who is who. We blend together to become more than two individuals'. "He allows me access to his most inner being; if he did not truly accept it was me, he would not allow the process. Give him my everlasting and enduring love as you, his friend, pass on my thoughts by putting vibrations on paper – the truth that I do exist – because by questioning himself, by default he questions me. I truly am Spirit and I will serve the divine to the best of my humble ability and if I find Bob's mind interfering in our communications I will withdraw and explain to him then or later, depending on the circumstances, what had occurred and how to avoid it in future. This is said to reassure him as I have every faith in him as my communicator to the physical. Shalom. Joshua."

—⁓—

Anne encouraged Bob to keep up the work and contact with 'a truly lovely man'.

T. H. Meyer, d. – 'Light for the new Millennium'

This is the title of a book edited by T. H. Meyer and published in German in 1993 and in English translation in 1997. As this book is of great significance to our theme, yet cannot be quoted out of context, the text of the cover page shall be given for the interest of anyone who might want to acquaint him/herself with its contents:

'Containing a wealth of crucial material on a variety of subjects, Light for the new Millennium is much more than a collection of previously unpublished letters and documents. It deals with themes which are of tremendous significance for our time, including; the end of the century and the new millennium; the future of Steiner's science of the spirit; karma and reincarnation; life after death; the working of evil; the destiny of Europe; and the hidden causes of the First World War. It also tells of the meeting of two great men and their continuing relationship beyond death: Rudolf Steiner (1861-1925) – seer. Scientist of the spirit, cultural innovator – and Helmuth von Moltke (1848-1916), Chief of the General Staff of the German army during the outbreak of the First World War.

Helmuth von Moltke first came into contact with Steiner through his wife Eliza, who was one of his esoteric pupils. In 1914, following disagreements with the Kaiser, Moltke was dismissed from his post. At this point Steiner's connection to the General – which included personal meetings as well as written communications – grew stronger. Although Moltke died two years later, Steiner kept in contact with his excarnated soul through clairvoyant means, and began to receive communications which were passed on to Eliza von Moltke. These messages – of supreme importance to the present – are reproduced here in full, together with the relevant letters of the General to his wife, and the 'document that could have changed world history'. –

Moltke's private reflections on the causes of the War, Steiner was prevented from publishing. Also included are a key interview with Steiner for le Matin and commentaries and essays by Juergen von Grone and Jens Heisterkamp, Johannes Tautz and an introduction and notes by T.H. Meyer.

Chapter 6

Rudolf Steiner,

The Science of the Spirit or Anthroposophy

Steiner was open to the question of reincarnation at an early stage of his life. In his autobiography he gives an impression of how life itself opened his eyes to this truth.

In 'The Story of my Life' he gives the following description: "I look upon the fact that I was privileged to know Fercher von Steinwand as one of the important events in my youth. The effect of his personality was that of a sage who reveals his wisdom in true poetry. I had been wrestling with the riddle of man's repeated earth lives. Many things about this problem became clearer through my close relation with people whose life-habits and personal characteristics clearly showed traces of individual traits which could not be explained by what had come through them by heredity or by experiences since birth. And in Fercher's case, every change of expression, every gesture revealed to me soul-qualities, which could only have been moulded when Greek paganism still influenced the development of Christianity at the beginning of the Christian era. Such insight cannot be gained by contemplating the more obvious and external characteristics of a person; rather one feels it arising when observing intuitively the more deeply individual traits that seemingly accompany the external characteristics. Nor is it any use to attempt to gain such insight while in the company of such a person; rather one must let a strong impression reverberate until it becomes like a vivid memory. Then what is considered significant in external life dissolves and the seemingly 'insignificant' begins to speak a clear language. One who 'observes' people in order to puzzle out their previous earth-lives will certainly not reach his goal. One must feel this as an offence against the person before one can hope that from a previous life, long past events will be revealed within the present, coming as it were from distant spiritual realms as if by an act of Providence."

Steiner was eager to apply the right method to his observation, he explains: 'Not by a cold observation and to prove one's own prejudice, which would be offensive, but by contemplating the after-image, then the seemingly insignificant characteristics "begin to speak a clear language". He continues:

"During this time I am now describing I gained through spiritual perception a definite insight into man's repeated earth-lives. Certainly, I had this insight before this time, but more in broad outlines, not in clearly defined impressions. I did not speculate about things like repeated earth-lives; I accepted it as something self-evident when meeting it in literature or in other ways but I did not theorise about it. It was because I was conscious of a direct insight into this sphere that made possible my conversation with Professor Neumann, referred to earlier. People who arrive at a conviction about the truth of repeated earth lives and similar things are certainly not to be blamed, for although direct knowledge of these facts can only be attained along supersensible paths, a perfectly valid conviction can be reached by healthy, unprejudiced common sense, even before the person has attained spiritual perception. It was just that in this sphere the theoretical path was not my path.

It was during this time when my spiritual perception in the sphere of repeated earth-lives became ever more clearly defined, that I came to know about the Theosophical Movement stemming from H. P. Blavatsky. A friend to whom I had spoken about these things sent me Sinnet's 'Esoteric Buddhism'. This book, the first I came across from the Theosophical Movement, did not impress me at all. But I was glad that I had not read it until after I had attained spiritual perceptions of my own. For to me its content was repellent, and my antipathy to such presentation of the super-sensible might well have prevented me in the first instance from pursuing further the path that had been outlined for me."

In his own development Rudolf Steiner pursued a philosophy which he later described in his book 'Philosophy of Freedom', or 'Spiritual Activity' as 'ethical individualism'. This is characterised by the emancipation from prejudices of all kinds and removes stumbling stones on the way for the acceptance of the idea of destiny and re-embodiment of the spirit.

Already in 1904 Steiner wrote in his book 'Theosophy' a chapter on 'Karma and Reincarnation' which gives a systematic description of the various salient components. But first, before presenting this, it will be instructive to have some excerpts from two lectures held in 1912, which gives a description of the spread of the Copernican theory even before proof was available. It was Rudolf Steiner's hope that the idea of repeated lives on earth should spread widely in the western world. He therefore took an interest in how the Copernican theory and system spread so quickly, even against the authority of the Church.

"What will be necessary in order that the concept of reincarnation and karma may comparatively soon instil itself into our education and take hold of human beings even in childhood, in the same way that children now are convinced of the truth of the Copernican theory of the universe. What was it that enabled the Copernican theory of the universe to lay hold of people's minds? This Copernican system had a peculiar destiny. I am not speaking about the theory itself but only about its entry into the world. Remember that this system was thought out by a Christian dignitary and that Copernicus's own conception of it was such that he felt it permissible to dedicate to the Pope the work in which he elaborated his hypothesis. He believed that his conclusions were entirely in keeping with Christianity. Was any proof of the truth of Copernicanism available at that time? Could anyone have demonstrated the truth of its conclusion? Nobody could have done so. But think of the rapidity with which it made its way into humanity. Since when has proof been available? To the extent to which it is correct, only the 1850's, only since Foucault's experiment with the pendulum. Before then there was no proof that the earth rotates. It is nonsense to state that Copernicus was able to prove what he had presented and investigated as a hypothesis; this also holds good of the statement that the earth rotates on its axis. Only since it was discovered that a swinging pendulum has the tendency to maintain the plane of its oscillation even in opposition to the rotation of the earth and that if a long pendulum is allowed to swing, then the direction of the oscillation rotates in relation to the earth's surface, could the conclusion be drawn: it is the earth beneath the pendulum that must have rotated. This experiment, which afforded the first actual proof that the earth moves, was not made until the 19th century. Earlier than that, there was no wholly satisfactory possibility as regarding Copernicanism as being anything more than a hypothesis. Nevertheless its effect upon the human mind in the modern age was so great that until the year 1822 this book was on the Index (the Catholic Church's list of prohibited books. This Index was formally abolished in 1966), in spite of the fact that Copernicus had believed it permissible to dedicate it to the Pope. Not until the year 1822 was the book, on which Copernicanism was based, removed from the Index – before any real proof of its correctness was available. The power of the impulse with which the Copernican theory of the universe instilled itself into the human mind finally compelled the Church to recognise it as non-heretical."

Steiner was acutely aware of these historical facts: ideas grown on Christian soil, dedicated to the head Christianity as it was then, being placed on the Index and then released because of popular demand, before they were fully tested. In the same lecture Steiner also points to the essential difference between the Copernican theory and the idea of reincarnation and karma:

"I have not spoken of Copernicanism without

reason. From the success of Copernicanism we can learn what will ensure the spread of the ideas of reincarnation and karma. What, then, were the factors responsible for the rapid spread of Copernicanism? I shall now say something terribly heretical, something that will seem quite atrocious to the modern mind. But what matters is that anthroposophy shall be taken as earnestly and as profoundly as Christianity was taken by the first Christians, who also arrayed themselves against the conditions prevailing. If anthroposophy is not taken with equal seriousness, by those who profess to be its adherents, it cannot achieve for humanity what must be achieved. I have now to say something quite atrocious, and it is this: Copernicanism, what we learn today as Copernican theory of the universe – the great merits of which and therewith its significance as a cultural factor of the very first order are truly not disputed – this theory was able to take root in human souls because to be a believer in this world system it is possible to be a superficial thinker. Superficiality and externality contribute to a more rapid conviction of Copernicanism. This is not to minimise its significance for humanity. But it can truly be said that people need not be very profound, need not deepen themselves inwardly, before accepting Copernicanism; they must far rather externalise their thinking. And indeed a high degree of externalisation has been responsible for trivial utterances such as those to be found in modern monistic books, where it is said, actually with a touch of fervour: compared with other worlds, the earth, as humanity's habitation, is a speck of dust in the universe. This is a futile statement for the simple reason that this 'speck of dust', with all that belongs to it, is of vital concern for human beings in terrestrial existence, and the other worlds in the universe with which the earth is compared are of less importance to us. The evolution of humanity was obliged to become completely externalised to be quickly capable of accepting Copernicanism. But what must people do to assimilate the teaching of reincarnation and karma? This teaching must meet with far more rapid success *if humanity is not to fall into decline.*[1] What is it that is necessary for the realising of the truth of reincarnation and karma? It is necessary to penetrate into intimate matters of the life of the soul, into things that every soul must experience in the deep foundations of its own core being. The results and consequences of Copernicanism in present-day culture are paraded everywhere nowadays, in every popular publication, and the fact that all these things can be presented in pictures – even, whenever possible, in films – is regarded as a very special triumph. This already characterises the tremendous externalisation of our cultural life. Little can be shown in pictures, little can actually be communicated about the intimacies of the truths we embraced in the words 'reincarnation' and 'karma'. To realise that the conviction of reincarnation and karma is well founded depends on a deepened understanding of such things as were said in the lecture yesterday. And so the very opposite of what is habitual in the external culture of today is necessary if the idea of reincarnation and karma is to take root in humanity. This is why such insistences laid upon this deepening – in the domain of anthroposophy too. Although it cannot be denied that certain schematic presentations may be useful for an intellectual grasp

---

1 Emphasis by author

of fundamental truths, it must nevertheless be realised that what is of primary importance in anthroposophy is to turn our attention to the laws operating in the depth of the soul, to what is at work inwardly, beneath the forces of the soul, as the outer, physical laws are at work in the worlds of time and space."

Over hundred years have passed since these words were spoken with a degree of urgency. On the one hand one can be disappointed that by comparison to the spread of Copernican system and the ideas of reincarnation and karma which have not yet become a cultural attribute of our time. On the other hand much has changed. Not only is it possible to speak openly about this idea: Many people carry it now with them as their personal conviction. The expanding work of past-life therapy helps considerably to make the idea popular, not just theoretically but by the real fruit it bears. The many calamities we face in our present time, will either make us ever more fearful and desperate by clinging to outer appearances, or they give us the opportunity to contemplate on the essentials of life and our own true being.

"We do not understand karma by talking in theoretical concepts about successive earthly incarnations. To understand karma is to feel in our hearts all that we can feel when we see what existed ages ago flowing into later epochs in the souls of men themselves. When we see how karma works, human life gains quite a new content. We feel ourselves quite differently in human life."

(From a lecture Rudolf Steiner given on 12th April, 1924)

—ᴍ—

Essential is the aspect of the deepening of the soul that Steiner points to. All that rests as memories in the 'unconscious,' rests in the depth of the soul. Not by self-absorbed brooding will we reach down to what is buried there, but by engaging in life and with our fellow-men in such a way that light can shine into this realm. Whilst bones, artefacts and effigies are being excavated from tombs and human structures of the past, there are also ways of researching the past by spiritual means through the individual who was a participant in mankind's many known and unknown civilizations of bygone ages. These are two parallel fields of research which require an expansion of consciousness as well as a sense of responsibility for each human being in the light of a wider horizon, and for the earth as our home planet.

As pointed out, Steiner gave a precise description of Reincarnation and Karma in a chapter in his earlier book 'Theosophy' (1904). There are currently so many misleading thoughts relating to the afterlife, to re-embodiment etc. that it is refreshing to read even today the spiritual-scientific clarity of concepts expressed by Rudolf Steiner already at the beginning of the 20th century.

—ᴍ—

Summery of the chapter 'Destiny and the Reincarnation of the Spirit' from 'Theosophy' with some linking comments in square ... brackets.

"The soul lives and acts in the middle ground between body and spirit. The impressions reaching the soul through the body are fleeting, present only as long as the body's organs are open to the things of the outside world... However what I recognise in my spirit as true... does not pass away with the present moment. The truth is not at all dependent on me... Whatever I may recognise through the spirit is grounded in an element of the soul's life that connects the soul to a universal content, a content that reveals itself within the soul but is independent of its transitory bodily basis. Whether this content is imperishable in every respect does not matter; what matters is that it be revealed in such a way that the soul's independent imperishable aspect, rather than its perishable bodily basis is involved. The soul's enduring aspect comes into view as soon as we become aware of experiences that are not limited by its transitory aspect. The soul preserves the present for remembrance, wresting it away from perishability and giving it a place in the permanence of its own spiritual nature... Through memory the soul preserves yesterday; through action it prepares tomorrow... Thus the life of the soul becomes a lasting consequence of the transitory impressions made by the outer world. But actions, too, acquire permanence once they have been stamped on the outer world". [Steiner gives the example of pruning a tree.] "What I have done today will remain in effect tomorrow... Is the 'I' not just as strongly linked to a change in the world that results from its own actions as is memory that results from an impression?... As an 'I' it enters into another relationship with the world that depends on whether it has carried out a certain action or another... I am a different person in my relationship to the world once I have made an impression on my environment... We must admit that something is now in the world as a result of our completed action, something whose character has been stamped on it by the 'I'. Thinking this through carefully, we arrive at a question: Could it be that the results of our actions, whose character has been impressed on them by our 'I', have a tendency to come back to the 'I' in the same way that an impression preserved in memory comes to life again when an outer circumstance evokes it? What is preserved in memory is waiting for a reason to reappear. Could it be the same with things in the outer world that have been made lasting by the character of the 'I'? Are they waiting to approach the soul from outside just as memory waits for a reason to approach from inside?" [What is posed here as a question is Steiner's conclusion:]

"As the keeper of the past, the soul is continually collecting treasures for the spirit. My ability to distinguish right from wrong is due to the fact that as a human being, I am a thinking being capable of grasping truth in my spirit. The truth is eternal; even if I were continually losing sight of the past and each impression were new to me, the truth could still always reveal itself to me again in things. But the spirit in me is not restricted to the impressions of the moment; my soul widens the spirit's field of vision to include the past. And the more my soul can add to the spirit from the past, the richer the spirit becomes. The soul passes on to the spirit what it has received from the body. Thus, at every moment of its life, the human spirit carries two different elements , the eternal laws of the true and the good; second, the recollection of past experiences. Whatever it does is accomplished under the influence of these two factors. Therefore, if we want to understand the human spirit, we must know two different things about it – first – how much of the eternal has been revealed to it, and second, how many treasures from the past it holds. These treasures do not remain in an unchanged form for the spirit." [Here followed the example of learning to read and write: The details of this process are forgotten, the ability remains.]

"Until now, we have been considering the spirit and the soul only between birth and death , but we cannot leave it at that." [Whereas much can be discovered within these two thresholds, the human Gestalt cannot be understood from heredity or from earthly forces and substances. It must have descended from another spiritual Gestalt.] "Human spiritual forms are as different as they can possibly be; no two individuals have the same spiritual form." Steiner appeals to sound observation, focusing on the spiritual aspect. "The physical similarity between human beings is apparent to the eye, and the difference between human spiritual forms is equally apparent to the unbiased spiritual view. This is demonstrated by one very evident fact – that human beings have biographies." [Just as members of a 'species' we could not have individual biographies, neither can animals have one. Only outer facts could be strung together but this would miss the point.] "What a human individual signifies, however, only begins where he or she stops being merely a member of a genus and species and becomes an individual being. … If we think about the nature of biography, we will realise that with regard to the spirit, each human being is his or her own individual genus." [This statement has core value in Steiner's science of the spirit.] "If a biographer captures a human being's uniqueness, it will be clear that this biography of one human being corresponds to the description of an entire animal species." [The question arises as to where this spiritual form, or Gestalt originates?] "As a spiritual human being, I have my own particular form, just as I have a personal biography. Therefore I cannot have acquired this form from anyone other than myself... I must have been present as a spiritual individual before my birth. I was certainly not present in my ancestors". [These ancestors show great differences. The conclusions drawn here are already an advance answer to the discovery of the genes and the practice of wanting to explain all individual traits by way of genetics. These apply to the body, not to the spirit.]

"I must – as a spiritual being – be the repetition of one whose biography can explain mine ... a spiritual individual must be a re-embodiment or reincarnation of one and the same spiritual being, for as a spiritual being, each person is his or her own species. We can object that what has been said here is a mere arrangement of thoughts, and we can demand external proof of it as we are accustomed to do in the case of ordinary science. However, it must be pointed out that the reincarnation of the spiritual human being is a process that does not belong to the domain of outer physical facts but takes place exclusively in the spiritual domain, and that of all our ordinary mental powers, only thinking has access to this realm. If we refuse to trust the power of thinking, we will never be able to explain higher spiritual facts to ourselves. But for anyone whose spiritual eye is open, the above train of though is just as compelling as any process taking place in front of our physical eyes. Those who find a so-called 'proof' constructed along the lines of ordinary scientific knowledge more persuasive than what has been presented about the significance of biography may well be a great scientist in the usual sense of the word, but they are far removed from the methods of true spiritual research".

[This full quotation was necessary because here is spelled out the method and the anthroposophical approach to the question of repeated lives on earth. The high value allotted to thinking shall not devalue other approaches where thinking is also of greatest importance. In the following aspects and terms are applied which have been dealt with in another chapter of 'Theosophy'. The body is described in three parts: the physical body, the life body and soul body. This part is closely linked to the first of three soul parts, the sentient soul. The third part, the consciousness soul is closely linked to the lowest part of the spirit, the spirit self. So much only as a pointer.]

"What has been presented so far provides the prerequisites for tracing our essential being beyond birth and death. Within the confines of birth and death, the human being belongs to the three words of bodily nature, soul nature and spirit nature. The soul forms the link between body and spirit by permeating the body's third member, the soul body, with the capacity for sensation and – as the consciousness soul – by pervading the first spiritual member, the spirit self. Throughout life, therefore the soul participates in both body and spirit, and this participation is expressed in all aspects of its existence. The organisation of the soul body determines to what extent the sentient soul can unfold its capacities; on the other hand, the consciousness soul's own life determines the extent to which the spirit self can develop within it. The better the body's development, the better the sentient soul can develop its interaction with the outer world; The more the consciousness soul supplies the spirit self with nourishment, the richer and more powerful the spirit self becomes. During life, this spirit self is supplied with this nourishment through worked-over and assimilated experiences, and through their fruits, as has been demonstrated. Naturally, this interaction between soul and spirit can take place only where the two intermingle, that is, in the joining of the spirit self and the consciousness soul." [There follows a more detailed description of the interaction of these border areas between soul and body and soul and spirit.]

"The spirit self brings the eternal laws of the true and good to the 'I' from the world of spirit. By means of our consciousness soul . These laws are linked to the soul's own individual life experiences. These experiences are transitory, but their fruits are lasting; the fact that they have been linked to the spirit self makes a lasting impression on it. If the human spirit approaches such an experience and finds it similar to another that it has already been linked to in the past, it recognises something familiar in it and knows that it must behave differently towards this than if it were encountering it for the first time. This is the basis of all learning. The fruits of learning are the abilities we acquire, and in this way, the fruits of our transitory life are imprinted on our immortal spirit." [The vague feelings of 'miracles' have become recognisable as the fruits of past lives efforts. From the point of view of spiritual science, the key is the individual human spirit.]

"In each life the human spirit appears as a

repetition of itself, with the fruits of its experiences in earlier lifetimes. ... Just as the life body reproduces the form of a species, the life spirit reproduces the soul from one personal existence to the next." [Steiner was fully aware of objections to the result of his research and was ready to hold his own ground, as the following sentence shows:] "And people who object that by conceiving an idea like this we could talk ourselves into believing in the reality of supersensible perception, only prove themselves incapable of really taking up the truth through independent thinking; they really talking themselves into believing their own objections."

[The last section of this chapter enlightens the reader about the nature of karma. Steiner points to the old comparison of death and sleep. When waking in the morning we pick up the situation we have left behind. Similarly at birth, not in outer similarity but both the inner disposition and outer happenings are not just accidental but have their affinity to the 'I'. The following quote specifies once more the three different realms to be considered:]

"The body is subject to the laws of heredity ; the soul is subject to self-created destiny or, to use the ancient term, to its karma; and the spirit is subject to the laws of reincarnation or repeated earthly lives. The interrelationship of body, soul and spirit can also be expressed as follows: The spirit is immortal; birth and death govern our bodily existence in accordance with the laws of the physical world; and the life of the soul, which is subject to destiny, mediates between body, soul and spirit during the course of an earthly life."

[A description of the three worlds is given in the

following chapter. The present chapter concludes with the sentence:]

"If our thinking comes to grips with life's phenomena and does not hesitate to follow thoughts resulting from living, vital observation through to their final ramifications, we can indeed arrive at the idea of repeated earthly lives and the law of destiny through mere logic. It is true that for the seer with opened spiritual eyes, past lives are present as a direct experience, like reading from an open book, but it is equally true that the truth of all of this can come to light for anyone with an active, observant reasoning ability."

In Conclusion: The reality of reincarnation and karma had a profound place in Rudolf Steiner's heart and thinking. In his work it constituted the background for everything. But he was sparing with referring to it. In his science of the spirit it was simply the basic factor. It found expression in his fundamental books and in his Mystery Plays and over hundred lectures. In these lectures he also drew attention to personalities in public life and history, but he used them as examples for certain developments and not as facts carved in stone. He was concerned to familiarise his audiences with the underlying principle, the working of karma. No doubt, religious feelings were evoked, but Steiner's approach was that of a scientist of the spirit. To those who were his more intimate students he gave detailed advice as to how they could enhance their faculties of remembering. The simplest of these exercises is the evening retrospective view of the day: to recall in all objectivity the events of the day in reverse order.

Whilst building his extraordinary life's work on the truth of repeated lives on earth, the gaze of his spirit had one focal point for all the history of mankind, earth and cosmos: This was the singular and unique incarnation of the Sun-spirit, Christ, in the man Jesus. For Steiner reincarnation went hand in hand with true Christianity. The next chapter tries to point to this important aspect. On the one hand Rudolf Steiner had the faculty of a lofty overview and penetration of mental problems, on the other hand he turned, when asked, to practical matters and aspects of life, such as social and religious renewal, education, special education, agriculture, medicine, economics, architecture and the arts. His knowledge was a one-man university, or better: The universe was reflected in the spirit of this man, focussed on the development of consciuosness and in the service of humanity and the earth in relation to the spirit.

Thomas H. Meyer – Rudolf Steiner's Core Mission

The book with above title ranks high in considering the theme of our book with a new look at Rudolf Steiner. Its substance is the methods and ways of gaining knowledge of former lives, neither by spontaneous remembering (mainly in young children) nor by employing hypnotic methods, nor by rational thinking. Spiritual science offers ways of methodical selfrecognition which can lead to certainties which are not subject to outer proofs. The author of this book stands on the grounds of the full acceptance of reincarnation and karma as a fact of life.

—◊◊—

In his Introduction Meyer describes two kinds of appreciation of Rudolf Steiner. The one kind of people see him as a child of his time and compare him in relation to other contemporaries and analyse the influences under which he lived and worked. The other kind of people seek to understand him as an abiding individuality in the stream of evolution. Meyer's book is avowed to the latter.

—◊◊—

Steiner never made any personal claims as regards personalities of the past in relation to himself. Yet people distant or close to him had certain impressions which they expressed. One such personality was a Catholic priest and professor, Wilhelm Anton Neumann, who, in Vienna, had listened to an early lecture by Steiner on 'Goethe as Father of a new Esthetics'. His remarks after the lecture proved of significance. Steiner's hints in the course of his life, always made in larger historical contexts, were veiled, yet some of his listeners woke up to such obscure indications. Meyer's book follows up many such observations in his line of enquiry and arrives at an astonishing answer. I shall, however, refrain speaking out of context, as, doing justice to Meyer's work, it is necessary to take into consideration the whole ambit of circumstances. Upon reading this book it becomes more understandable why Steiner experienced reincarnation and karma, from childhood on, as self-evident.

—◊◊—

Meyer's work sees Steiner's core mission in pointing to the fact that great individualities have a mission in the evolution and history of mankind, spanning over many incarnations. Examples are given which also underlie certain descriptions in the Gospels. This reference can therefore serve as a link to the next chapter.

Chapter 7

Reincarnation in Christianity

Geddes MacGregor –
Reincarnation in Christianity

Geddes MacGregor, Emeritus Distinguished Professor of Philosophy at the University of Southern California has chosen the above title for his book, published in 1978. He received numerous awards over the years and was the first holder of the Rufus Jones Chair in Philosophy and Religion at Bryn Mawr. The book presents 'A New Vision of the Role of Rebirth in Christian Thought'.

This work was positively received by leading personalities across the religious divides. The following is more than a book review and requires some text quotations and the acknowledgement of the author's independent and comprehensive knowledge. – Yet there are also a number of questions he did not raise, nor answer satisfactorily. Some commentaries from the viewpoint of Rudolf Steiner's work will be added, as no direct reference is made to his research.

Geddes MacGregor presents his views with great circumspection and deals with the host of historical and contemporary views, also of other religions, with great erudition. He has researched the relevant Church Councils and influential person-alities, showing up many human shortcomings and biases which still inform present attitudes. He stresses that reincarnation, re-embodiment is not a religion, nor in contradiction with the Christian Faith and, towards the end of his book, shows open ways for its integration. It will be shown, that several of the obsta-cles can be removed through Rudolf Steiner's insights.

MacGregor's starting point is the range of ideas of reincarnation and karma in our time. His chief question is their compatibility with the Christian Faith and finds among the Church Fathers several who held this view with conviction. Above them all, Origen, whom he considers the greatest, an 'intellec-tual giant', who was wronged by jealous colleagues and finally condemned by the Council of Alexandria in 400 AD. For Origen there was a way to see rein-carnations as stepping stones towards resurrection. He held as the highest ideals the 'love of God and human freedom'. He also had the notion of 'pure spirit, suc-cessive lives and permanent instability'. MacGregor concludes: "What is certain and may be tragic, is, that that Christians have since generally believed (for not everyone can be expected to know of the muddle, obscurity and inconclusiveness of the politico-ecclesi-astical proceedings) that reincarnation is incompati-ble with Christian Faith. They have taken for granted, therefore, that it is a forbidden notion, to embrace that which is to renounce Christ and to abandon the Church, which is his Body. They have supposed, from what they have either read or heard from bishops, priests, and others on whom they have been accus-tomed to depend, that the Fifth Ecumenical Council had closed the door for ever. As already noted in an earlier chapter, both the Council of Lyons in 1274 and the Council of Florence in 1439 simply assume that reincarnationism (which by that time had appeared as a prominent tenet of the indubitably heretical Albigenses) had been long ago outlawed"

Questions from this early time have remained throughout the Middle Ages, and are still with us, such as the time after death: the limbo, purgatory, hell and heaven, and whether they are places, or states of being. The question of pure spirit remains a vital question, also to Professor MacGregor.

The epitaph for the chapter on the Renaissance and later literature is a quote by Lord Dowding, renowned for his part in the Battle of Britain: "I am personally convinced beyond any shadow of doubt that reincarnation is a fact". The chapter gives a collection of renowned names, not only of poets, but also prominent people in public life, such as Henry Ford, Lloyd George, Benjamin Franklin. Among the poets appear the names of Walt Whitman, Flaubert, W.B. Yeats, John Mansfield, Coleridge, Dryden, Longfellow and several others. This list is by no means complete and shows that it is not just a trickle, but a current of personal convictions. Among the humanistic thinkers of the Renaissance in Italy, MacGregor mentions Pico della Mirandola and especially Giordano Bruno who had entered the Dominican Order as a boy of fifteen. For his 'heretic' views he later was burned on the stake in Rome in 1600 AD.

The chapter 'Which is the Self' shows under which materialistic strain the author has laboured. By definition he eliminated all the transient symptoms that outwardly define a person. He says: "I can wipe

out whole areas of myself that I had taken to be insep-
arable from all this I call 'me' and yet retain a vigorous
sense of identity. Yet the self seems to remain unfathomable. The term is, to say the least, ambiguous. How
could I so empty myself as to leave nothing for my
friends to recognise as me, yet re-enter another womb
and live again?"

In this critically essential point, the spiritual
science of Rudolf Steiner can provide fundamental
insights. Steiner looks upon the "I", as the most human,
objective and independent manifestation of the self. It
works already as a force of energy in the building up
of the upright human form in the embryo, right into
the vertical structure of the skeleton, and influencing
the immune-system which rejects foreign bodies. The
"I" is also at work in (the body of) personal habits, dis-
played in time. It is further the controller of desires,
emotions, joys and sorrows of the soul or Astral body.
These three constituents of the human being, over
which the "I" exerts control, are akin to the mineral
world, occupying space and giving form; – the living,
quasi sleeping plant world, with its vegetative habits
of growth and decay, – and the animal kingdom, with
its variety of passions, and its enhanced, dreamlike
consciousness and mobility. – Conceiving the self, the
"I" in these terms enables a clear thinking to free itself
from the constrains of holding on to outer criteria.
We find this human "I" already invisible during life,
yet expressing itself in this threefold way, through,
what Rudolf Steiner calls 'physical body', 'ether,- or
life-body' and 'astral body'. This insight has a bearing
on how to imagine the situation after death when the
"I" has lost it's mediator to the natural environment
with the loss of the body. Then the "I" is admitted to

a spiritual environment which, according to Steiner, is even more real. We can also be reminded of some passages from the Gospel of St. John and the letters of Paul which refer to this topic of self and different bodies.

In Chapter 3 of the Gospel of St John, Nicodemus asks the question: "How can a man be born when he is old, can he enter a second time into his mother's womb?" Jesus answered, "Very truly, I say to you, unless one is born of water and the Spirit, he cannot enter the Kingdom of God. That which is born of the flesh is flesh, and that which is born of the Spirit is spirit. Do not marvel that I said to you 'You must be born again.'"

This is not taken as an instruction referring to re-embodiment, but it refers to a kingdom of God without which reincarnation is unthinkable and presupposes that the "I", or self, has the innate ability, or potential to be reborn –.

It is surprising that, regarding the time after death, Mac Gregor refers to so many obstacles in accepting Paul's teaching (1st Corinthians, Chapter 15 verse 40 +) of the difference of terrestrial, and celestial (spiritual) bodies, who by necessity, must live in a spiritual environment.

"There are also celestial bodies and terrestrial bodies; but the glory of the celestial bodies is one, and the glory of the terrestrial body is another. ... It is sown a natural body, it is raised a spiritual body. ... And so it is written, "The first man Adam became a living being". The last Adam became "a life-giving spirit".

This is also in tune with words Jesus Christ spoke to the Samaritan woman (John Chapter 4 verses 21-24:

"Woman, believe me, the hour is coming when you will neither on this mountain, nor in Jerusalem, worship the Father. You worship what you do not know; we know what we worship. ... But the hour is coming, and now is, when the true worshippers will worship the Father in spirit and truth; for the Father is seeking such to worship him. God *is* Spirit, and those who worship him must worship in spirit and truth." (Both the Greek and Latin have no article before Spirit; 'Spiritus est Deus').

In his chapter 'Mysticism V Faith' Geddes MacGregor expresses the strong view that both are incompatible. If, however, with Paul, we accept that the 'last Adam' is a life-giving spirit, then even human beings can receive in their spirit, the "I", a spark of the divine fire, which is love, or a drop from the ocean of God's creativity, the recognition of it can be received as a gift of grace in humility. Then this is no longer a teaching or article of faith, but an experience of the heart which can rightly be called 'mystical'. This also applies to words of Christ (John 15.4) "Abide in me, and I in you". The gulf to which MacGregor refers between man and God in Judaism, Islam and Christianity, overlooks the fact that this gulf has been bridged by Christ becoming Man in Jesus. He told his disciples (John 15.15) "No longer do I call you servants, for a servant does not know what his master is doing; but I have called you friends, for all things that I have heard of my Father I have made known to you". The personal experience of the truth of these words can be seen as a deeply Christian mysticism, and how should this be anathema?

Geddes MacGregor struggles with the right understanding of the soul where in some religious views the soul is considered eternal which he dismisses as soul-stuff, but gives recognition to the achievements of the soul's endeavour during life. Here again, Steiner's differentiation between soul and spirit draws a clear line. The following passage from his early publication 'Theosophy', gives a concise description of this interconnection:

"The course of human life within the framework of birth and death is determined in three different ways, and we are also dependent on three factors that go beyond birth and death. The body is subject to the laws of *heredity;* the soul is subject to self-created destiny or, to use an ancient term, to *karma;* and the spirit is subject to the laws of *reincarnation* or repeated earthly lives. The interrelationship of body, soul and spirit can also be expressed as follows: The spirit is immortal; birth and death govern our bodily existence in accordance with the laws of the physical world; and the life of soul, which is subject to destiny, mediates between body and spirit during the course of an earthly life. These three worlds to which we belong will be the subject of the next section of this book, since some familiarity with them is a prerequisite for all further knowledge of the essential nature of the human being."

The sixteenth and last chapter (A New Vision Of The Afterlife) bears the epitaph from John 14.2, "In my Father's house are many mansions... I go to prepare a place for you." These are the same words used as book titles by Lord Dowding and Dr Gina Cerminara, in which she describes the well-known clairvoyant seer and healer, Edgar Cayce, who also was a dedicated Christian.

The following quotations present a summery of Geddes MacGregors findings: "If one is not persuaded of the possibility of some kind of afterlife, no logical conclusion or scientific method could conceivably lead to belief in it. Such a conclusion can spring only from faith. Nevertheless, the man or woman who walks in faith rightly seeks to articulate that faith intelligibly. The extraordinary muddled state of traditional Christian eschatology serves only to perplex those who so live by Christian faith. Our task is to provide a more intelligible account of that to which Christian faith and hope point. ... Wherever there is a slight stirring of the spirit of man, a movement, however feeble, toward a fuller life, a flow, however trickling, of compassion and human understanding, or even so much as a desperate ambition to get somehow beyond the prison of one's own circumstances and the strait-jacket of one's own mind., then another chance is what one would expect of the God of love. Even the most rigorous professional examinations, which impose strict time-limits, provide for more than one chance. In case of failure, one may try again. Christian tradition has recognised such a notion in the Catholic doctrine of purgatory, surely one of the most consoling as well as morally invigorating doctrines in all Christian teaching."

"The doctrine of purgatory, emerging as it did in a mass of mental confusion about the destiny of man, was vague and ambiguous from the start. Even for those simple souls who thought of heaven as a shining city in the sky approached by pearly gates, paved with gold and watered by crystal rivers, as they thought of hell as a burning dungeon below, the concept of purgatory was inchoate. Sometimes people thought of it as a pale version of hell; but then they saw that would not do, because, being a correctional rather than penal institution, every flame has a cleansing and clarifying purpose. ... Nothing can ever be accomplished in hell. For purpose itself has been for ever abolished. Then, to the eyes of faith, purgatory is a pilgrimage much more like that of this life than either heaven or hell could ever be... Apart from the prejudices against reincarnationism that we have already considered, a further theological objection must have presented itself to the thoughtful. The resurrection of the dead was generally supposed to take place "in the end "when the whole universe was about to be "rolled up like a scroll and time itself about to terminate. ... Yet the notion of such a condition of spiritual disembodiment was as alien to the Aristotelian philosophy and science of the Middle Ages as it is to contemporary science and philosophy. So purgatory remained the fuzzy notion it had ever been and the Latin mania for legalistic definition served only to aggravate the fuzziness."

There follow several pages in which MacGregor compares the views held in the past and in different religions regarding the further development and a final redemption or bliss, before he arrives at his final assessment and expresses his personal views as follows:

"That individuality, that personality that is leaping out of what is superficially called "me" is the energy in me that cannot die and must find embodiment, perhaps many thousands of times before "the end of the age". The energy is immortalised by the peculiar direction it has taken. It is not energy that is spent in exercise of power, for that kind of energy, though it may play a part in the moral development of the individual, is burnt up like any other form of energy. It is, on the contrary, the energy that is created by the abdication of power. Hence the Gospel paradox: "He that findeth his life shall lose it; and he that loseth his life for my sake shall find it." Love, which entails sacrifice, the abdication of self-centred power, immortalises energy by putting it into the trusteeship of God. So self-renunciation, far from inhibiting me, enables me, rather, "to turn again and live." (referring to the Swiss physician and psychotherapist, Paul Tournier, '*The Meaning of Persons*') "I see no reason why a Christian should not at least entertain the suggestion that the re-embodiment should occur over and over again, giving the individual opportunity to grow in the love of God. That re-embodiment I would call reincarnation. I am inclined to think the concept of reincarnation is, indeed, the key to a fuller understanding of human destiny. Of course primitive forms of reincarnationism must be discarded. In the history of religious ideas, outmoded formulations are continually giving place to more adequate ones. The temptation of throwing the baby out with the bath water is familiar, however, to all historians of ideas, religious or otherwise. Religious revolutionaries often succumb to it; but so even more do those ideophobiacs who hug ancient formulations till they petrify, yet will not tolerate the new formulations that could restore and develop religious life. Could it not be that reincarnationism, which has taken such well-known primitive forms, might have been a particularly unfortunate casualty?"

"I see myself drawn forth in the course of my present life from the amorality of self-centredness to a much deeper sense of the love of God, with the peculiar kind of moral vivacity that such a development always brings. I remember vividly the prison of that self-centeredness and know so well how far the grace of God has taken me in my struggle for freedom. Yet for all the vast progress I see, I know I have farther to go than I can hope to go in this life.

Each reincarnation is, of course, a resurrection. The resurrection that is promised to those who are partakers of the resurrection of Christ is not only preserved as the Christian hope; it can now be seen as a continuing process in which every rebirth gives me new capacity for walking closer and closer toward God".

Geddes MacGregor still considers other aspects of this 'amazing grace' that has opened to him these great vistas and he concludes his book by saying, "We may conclude that there is nothing in biblical thought or Christian tradition that necessarily excludes all forms of reincarnationism. We have seen many historical reasons why it must be in conflict with the historic teachings that have come to us through the Bible and the Church. We have seen, above all, that some form of reincarnationism could much enhance the spirituality of the West, not least at the present time when it stands so much in need of fresh avenues of development and new means of illumination."

The present writer could not agree more with these thoughts and sentiments expressed by Professor Geddes MacGregor, but finds it hard to understand that a person of such a wide scope of knowledge and insight, has appreciated so little what Rudolf Steiner has put forward as his spiritual research of the realities adressed with the words 'karma and reincarnation'. Rudolf Steiner answers to all the criteria that are needed to enhance the spirituality of the West, indeed he can illuminate all the spiritual and social life of humanity.

From a conventional Christian point of view it is obvious that Steiner's views do not converge easily with strongly held traditional views. Yet a highly regarded Canon, Dr A P Shepherd, has made an earnest study of Steiner's work and describes his views in the following essay, published in New York in 1963. These new views could, with a measure of good will, open doors for a wider and deeper appreciation of Christian values and insights both now and into the future.

A. P. Shepherd, D. D. – Anthroposophy and the Christian Churches

The following essay Dr. Shepherd wrote and published in New York in an anthroposophical magazine. As it gives a comprehensive view of his thinking, the whole essay is reprinted here.

ANTHROPOSOPHY AND THE
CHRISTIAN CHURCHES

Although it is sixty years since Rudolf Steiner first began to expound his world-picture of the fundamental reality of spirit as the primary creative force throughout the universe, his teaching has been almost unnoticed by the Christian Churches. In its early stages this was largely accounted for by the historical situation. The birth of Anthroposophy at the opening of the twentieth century was historically a surprising phenomenon. Science, in the first flush of its confident development of the Darwinian theory of evolution, was complacently asserting the sufficiency of matter and its functions to explain the whole universe, including man him-self. The first violent orthodox reaction against the Darwinian theory had died down, and public opinion was gradually accepting the scientific view-point as proved. On the continent, and especially in Germany, where Haeckel's version of Darwinism had swept the board, Protestant theologians were humanizing Christianity, extracting from it almost everything that was supernatural. In the Protestant Churches of England and America theology was at a low ebb, and there was a complacent indifference to the apparent contradiction between credal and scientific beliefs, in the confident expectation that the world was getting better and better every day.

It was amazing that at that moment of complacent materialism, a young Austrian scientist, under the impulse of his own highly-developed supersensible faculties and of an over-mastering experience of Christ, should begin to expound factually the spirit background of man and the universe, and the working of spirit from the very beginning of creation, through the whole evolutionary process, up to its continuous immediate activity in the kingdoms of nature and in man. Moreover, that he should place at the pivotal point of this cosmic evolutionary process the person and earthly life of Christ, and expound in their full supernatural significance the recorded incidents of his life that so many theologians were engaged in explaining away. The first of his series of lectures and publications was an exposition of the full significance of the redemptive deed of Christ in the spiritual world-setting, and this was shortly followed by a similar treatment of the four Gospels.

In his deliberately undertaken life-work of expounding the reality of spirit and its universal working it was almost inevitable that Steiner was at first brought into close contact with the Theosophical Movement, for that was the only movement at that time that was consciously based on the immediate apprehension of spirit reality. From the commencement this association was somewhat strained, for the Theosophical Movement sought its inspiration in the ancient spirit-wisdom of the East, while Steiner revealed spirit-knowledge as a new possibility of the present age, through the metamorphosis of the powers of thought which were the main-spring of western scientific progress. Moreover, Steiner's unswerving assertion of the crowning finality of the deed of Christ was distasteful to the Theosophical viewpoint which saw all religions as equally a manifestation of divine truth. In a few years, the Theosophical leaders could no longer tolerate this deep division of approach within their Society, and Steiner carried on his task independently under the title of Anthroposophy or Spiritual Science.

This movement was almost entirely confined to the Continent, but there Steiner travelled from country to country and from place to place in an almost ceaseless round of lectures, given to ever-increasing audiences of those who were seekers after the spirit. His great appeal was that he spoke out of direct perception of supersensible reality, and also fully expounded the methods by which ordinary human consciousness might acquire that faculty. He had just completed the full exposition of the spirit-nature of man and the universe, when, like an unexpected clap of thunder out of blue skies, the first World War shattered the complacency of mankind.

After the war, Steiner proceeded to establish his teaching by applying its principles to all departments of human life and social activity, and in those years he visited England and made a deep impression upon some of its leading thinkers. The Churches, however, were still impervious to his message. Only the Church of Rome, with its invariable opposition to any spiritual revelation that had not its immediate source in its own authority, showed open hostility to Anthroposophy. The other Churches in Germany were still too busy trimming revelation to the accepted scientific pattern, while to the Churches of England and America it was unknown or, at best, a strange foreign "ism".

In 1925 Rudolf Steiner died, and his followers, stunned by the loss of his personality, took a considerable time to organise and make effective their propagation of his work. To-day, however, Anthroposophy is a world-wide Movement and has imposed itself deeply on many departments of human life. Nevertheless, to-day, over forty years after Steiner's death, it remains almost unknown to and unnoticed by the Christian Churches. If this seemed strange at the beginning of the century, it is all the more amazing now, when the Churches are facing crises and problems in all directions. At the dawn of the Russian revolution in 1917, Dr. Steiner foretold the cataclysmic changes which would follow it, especially after the middle of the century. One after another they have occurred, National-Socialism, race-persecution, a second World War, an ordered and defiant political materialism which captures whole peoples, a cold war which toys with the menace of world destruction, and, above all a Science, which no longer concerns itself chiefly with the natural relationships between Earth and Man, but has penetrated to a sub-human level, at which, with brain washing, human processing, and artificial insemination, it denies or would destroy the spiritual being of man.

There are some Church leaders who comfort themselves with the fact that there is an increase in Church attendance in the last decade. This is undeniable, especially in the U.S.A., and there is no doubt that the uncertainty of the world-situation is driving many to the assurance and comfort of a gospel of personal salvation. No-one would deny or belittle the value of this personal attitude to Christianity, but its real effectiveness for humanity is in the measure in which it penetrates the every-day concepts of life in the world. A leading American writer in a recent interview declared that although perhaps 75% of the American people attended some place of worship on Sunday, during their week-day life almost all of them accepted unquestioningly the materialistic scientific interpretation of man and the universe.

There, in the enormous prestige of a materialistic Science, dominating, absorbing, fascinating the human mind, and especially that of the rising generation, is the problem that confronts the Christian Churches. To Science, with its astounding advances and almost daily breath-taking discoveries and anticipated possibilities, the Christian Faith is irrelevant, a possible solace to the individual, but of no vital significance to the evolutionary past or future of humanity, and, still less, of the universe. Personal religion will lack force, if indeed it can survive, with this divided outlook. The answer to it, is not to bring religious faith more into line with scientific opinion, though that seems to be the objective of a certain type of theology. It is to see whether a deeper consideration of the factual findings of scientific observation will lead to conclusions consistent with Christian belief. It would appear that it is the scientist himself, rather than the theologian, who doubts the certainty of scientific conclusions. Pierre Teilhard de Chardin is a Jesuit priest, but in *The Phenomenon of Man*, his penetrating criticism of scientific materialism, he writes as a scientist.

But more directly menacing to the Churches than the theoretical materialism of Science is the deliberate hostility of the powerfully organised social and political system of Communism, based upon a complete denial of spirit in man and the universe. Already it dominates two-fifths of the human race and it expands by ceaseless and ruthless propaganda. It can only be effectively countered by proving the reality of spirit and manifesting the nature of its working at every level of being.

Yet another problem that confronts world-Christianity is the rapidly increasing racial and national consciousness in the non-white peoples. It manifests itself in a deep antipathy to European and American domination. The Christian religion, which perforce has been propagated under the forms of its western historical evolution, is coming to be regarded as a foreign importation, and the revival of the indigenous religion as a symbol of independent self-development.

Finally, there is a problem that only came to the fore three years ago by the publication in 1963 of the Bishop of Woolwich's book, "Honest to God," which has received great publicity and a considerable measure of approval. This problem is all the more serious inasmuch as it has had its source within the Christian Churches themselves. It is an attempt to bridge the gulf between members of the Christian Churches and those who, while accepting the moral and social standards of Christianity, are unable to accept many of its credal statements and forms of worship. This movement, which calls itself "Religionless Christianity", seeks to create the bridge by accepting as proved the scientific world outlook of today, and bases itself upon the alleged fact that "this generation has opted for the secular and has done with the supernatural". Such an approach to the problem is the very antithesis of that of Rudolf Steiner, with his revelation of the reality of the supersense-perceptible, and its essential relevance to the Deed of Christ, to the Christian Gospel, and to the Destiny of Man.

To all these problems Anthroposophy has specific answers, but it has received no serious consideration by the Churches. It is either casually dismissed by the traditional theological substitute for impartial judgement, as "the revival of a long disproved heresy"; or it is rejected on the ground of some startling or unfamiliar item of belief, taken out of its context, and with no consideration or even knowledge of the basic principles on which it rests.

In point of fact, the Churches are not to-day so completely averse to supersensible phenomena as they were at the beginning of the century and they regard with sympathetic interest the study, under approved control, of spiritualism and spirit-healing. But these movements provide only empirical evidence of spirit reality, and the rationale of their belief is very largely speculation. It is all the more surprising that the Churches should show no interest in Anthroposophy, a rationally articulated world-outlook, based on the reality and activity of spirit and derived from direct perception. This perception is based upon the development of inherent organs of supersensible perception by methods which are exactly described, and which involve penetration in full consciousness into different levels of soul experience, factually linked with each other. In the understanding of these levels of experience we arrive at the understanding of the great mysteries of man and of space and time.

In speaking of the Christian Churches I have deliberately made no reference to "The Christian Community", for that Church came into being in 1922 as the expression in a Christian Church of the teaching of Anthroposophy, in despair at the indifference and opposition of the traditional Churches. This Church has a large membership in Germany; in English-speaking countries it is small, but quietly and steadily growing. It manifests a new understanding of the Christian verities in the light of Anthroposophy. But for the traditional Christian Churches the path of discovery of the message of Anthroposophy is not, at first, through its direct interpretation of Christian doctrine, whether in the practice and worship of the Christian Community, or in Dr. Steiner's lectures on the Gospels and on the life and work of Jesus Christ. To do that is to be confronted immediately with statements that may seem to contradict long-accepted views, without any knowledge of the principles on which they are based.

Through his direct experience of spirit and by thorough penetration of this experience by clear thought and honest judgement, Steiner arrived at certain fundamental principles that underlie the whole of man and the universe. Some of these are new, some are a clarification of ancient instinctive knowledge. Some of them challenge accepted scientific and theological conceptions, but they do so in a scientific way. Steiner urged repeatedly that none of these principles should be accepted on authority, but that they should be tested, either by developing in oneself the power of direct spirit-perception, or by submitting them to the most searching tests in the light of existing indisputable factual knowledge. They are, however, so fundamental to his whole world-outlook that it is only comprehensible in the light of them. Moreover, if they are true, they so vitally concern the thinking and life of humanity, that nothing can be more important than an honest consideration of them.

The first principle is the apprehension of the objective reality of spirit, a vast, inter-related super-sensible world of spirit-being, existing behind and functioning through material reality, the Alpha and Omega of physical, sense-perceived existence. Such a concept should not be unfamiliar to Christians, who speak in their services every Sunday of "Cherubim and Seraphim", "the heavens and all the powers therein". In spite of this, however, any real living relationship to heavenly spirit is almost nonexistent in their minds. Natural Science is governed by the principle of not treating as factual anything that is not capable of being proved by sense-perceptible experiment, but already there is a gathering mass of evidence of events that do not admit of a scientific explanation of this sort. Moreover, if such a world of spirit does exist, it cannot, by its very nature, be subject to sense-derived proof.

The second principle that runs through the whole relation between the spiritual and the physical worlds is that of "Descent and Ascent". For the past hundred years Science has been fascinated by and absorbed in the picture of "Ascent" manifest in the physical world. With varying views as to the motive power in this ascent, the picture remains as a process which had its origin in the lowest physical forms and will have its conclusion in the highest. But Dr. Steiner has revealed the whole process as a continuous "descent" of spirit into matter, shaping first its own being in the supersensible world to the needs of descent, and then evolving a material medium which it progressively shaped more and more adequately to its self-manifestation in physical form. The natural scientific approach is like that of examining the pictures of a great painter, and deciding how they could be arranged in an order of objective artistic merit, and what explanation could be given from the pictures themselves of their artistic advance. It would be seen as a manifest "ascent". The Anthroposophical approach would be to regard the pictures as the progressive "ascending" expression of the artist's creative imagination continually "descending" into pictorial form, how he trained his imagination towards self-expression and by adaptation and new discovery he made his material more and more capable of expressing his genius, a process of descent and ascent continuously repeated at every stage of advance. Whenever there is life in the physical world this process is continuously repeated, in a rhythm of descent ascent and withdrawal; and where, in man, spirit itself completely and consciously descends into the material medium, the process resolves itself into the next great principle that is fundamental to Anthroposophy; the principle of reincarnation, or successive earth-lives.

The belief in reincarnation is one to which the Christian Churches are instinctively opposed, partly because it is not an explicit element in the teaching of Christ, and partly because it has long been regarded as one of the mistaken beliefs of Eastern religions. In point of fact the Eastern conception of reincarnation is quite different from that presented in Anthroposophy. The Eastern religions, based as they were on a primeval human clairvoyance, spoke out of a direct perception of a previous existence. But to them man's lives on earth are a calamity, an exile from his true spirit-existence, and he seeks to bring to an end their repetition by asceticism. But Dr. Steiner explains reincarnation as the necessary application to the individual man of the principle of descent and ascent manifest in the whole universe. It is the spiral of spiritual evolution, by which man is enabled by purgation and spiritual re-integration finally to carry the purpose of his earthly incarnation into pure spirit-existence. In recent years, there has been among Western people a growing interest in the possibility of reincarnation, but it has tended to concentrate all interest and importance on the repeated earth lives, and to fail to realise the process as a great rhythm of being, in which the earth-lives are held together in an unbroken chain of moral consequence, the goal of which lies in the spiritual world.

It is impossible within the scope of this article to consider the relevance of this belief to the Christian Faith, why it was necessary that for nearly two thousand years, while man was achieving an ever deeper knowledge of himself and his material environment, it should be hidden from his consciousness; how vitally important that at this moment in his evolution he should recover that knowledge; how deeply relevant to its needs is the redeeming work of Christ; how it answers many of the apparently inscrutable inequalities of human life and opportunity; and how significant to each one of us it makes, not only our own present earthly existence, but the whole history of man and the earth. Indeed, if reincarnation is true there is no fact that is more vitally urgent to-day for man to apprehend. It leads directly to the next fundamental principle of Anthroposophy, the nature of the being of man in his earthly existence.

The concept of the nature of man governs the thinking and the life of humanity. The greatest menace of our age is the utterly false view of man implicit in materialistic science, and blatantly explicit in Marxian Communism. In Spiritual Science earthly man is seen as a physical-spiritual being. His eternal self, which moves as spirit through this repeated rhythm of being, dwells in each earth-life in a soul-element of thinking, feeling and willing that it has fashioned out of its earth-existences; in a life-element, that brings it from spirit life to conscious inner experience in a continuous time-existence, and finally, in a physical body, a controlled spatial existence, in which alone man can realise himself in moral freedom. Dr. Steiner shows the interplay of these elements in man's being on earth, both when awake and asleep, and in the spiritual life after death.

In one sense this revelation of the true being of man is the very core of the revelation of Rudolf Steiner, as is implicit in the strange-sounding name of his movement. For "Anthroposophy" is the wisdom attained through the discovery of the true nature of man. For the Church it must be of vital importance, for, as we said earlier, there is a widespread tendency to-day to combine a profession of Christian faith with the modern scientific view of man.

This true view of man was unconsciously and only partially present in ancient religions, but since the time of Aristotle man has lost any direct awareness of it. In the first three centuries of Christianity an attempt was made to express the Christian faith in terms of it , but from the fourth century it faded away. It is not too much to say that most of the great theological disputes which have torn the Church asunder since that time have been due to the ignorance on both sides of the true nature of man.

This understanding leads directly to the next great principle explicit in Anthroposophy, the meaning of History. This is a problem which has pressed urgently upon men's minds in the last fifty years. Here again Dr. Steiner saw the working of this great principle of "Descent and Ascent". Here the rhythm is as long as the whole course of human evolution. Slowly man descended from an unself-conscious spirit existence, into gradual incarnation into a material existence. More and more deeply the human race has penetrated into material knowledge and experience, with a corresponding loss of awareness of spirit. From that depth man is slowly ascending, but for that he needs a reawakened spiritual consciousness. The question for our day is whether that consciousness will be blinded by the dazzling splendour of man's latest material discoveries.

The external course of history, the rise and fall of civilisations, the gradual advance in physical knowledge and power from the Stone Age to the Atomic Age, are only half the tale of human history, and can only be properly understood as an element in man's spiritual devolution and evolution. In this long slow rhythm, the quicker rhythm of the individual is not only the necessary condition whereby he may survive the stress and incomprehensibility of the slower movement, but provides, through the return of the spiritually-quickened power of great lives, the impulse which leads to new civilisations.

Perhaps the most striking point and the one most relevant to the Christian Churches is the place which Dr. Steiner gave in this cosmic view of history to the Deed of Christ, the Incarnation. To him it was not only the intervention of God into human history, bringing forgiveness and the hope of immortality to the individual believer, and drawing out a redeemed community from a doomed world. It was the central point of all human history, occurring at the very nadir of mankind's spiritual descent, and bringing new spiritual forces and creative possibilities for the whole future of the spiritual destiny of man. He saw the incarnation not as a sudden deed erupting into history, but as a gradual descent through the levels of existence from spirit to matter, a descent of which great human spirits were aware at different levels and which they expressed in the great religions of mankind, but which found its fulfilment only in Christ. This picture of the Cosmic Christ, the Christ of human destiny, can be the answer to the new race-prejudice, which sees Christianity as a Western ideology.

Anthroposophy proclaims to human thinking the objective and immediate reality of spirit. It also restores to the study of Christian documents and origins the reality of the supersensible. In its light the Bible takes on a new spiritual and rational meaning, the accounts of the Creation and the Fall, the call of Abraham and the segregation of the Hebrew people, the task of Moses, the nature of prophecy, the deep significance of the Exile, the Messianic expectation. So too the New Testament, the deep mystic significance of the four Gospels in their varied presentation, the meaning of Apocalypse. This new understanding of the Bible, based on the teaching of Rudolf Steiner, has been set out with great erudition and spiritual insight by the late Dr. Emil Bock of the Christian Community, in his studies on the Old and New Testaments.

But the chief possibility that lies in an unprejudiced approach to Anthroposophy by the Christian Churches is that with which we began, a real reconciliation of Science and Religion. If the Church can see the work of Christ and the spiritual destiny and redemption of man as involved in the whole evolutionary process; and if Science can see the evolutionary process in the light of its spiritual origin, nature and destiny; then it might begin to happen. That was the task to which Rudolf Steiner devoted his life.

Nineteen centuries ago Saul of Tarsus, a gifted man of about forty, deeply versed in the culture and religious thought of his age, yet wholly committed to the most definite and uncompromising religion of the world, the Jewish faith, had a vision of Christ. As a result of the spiritual initiation which flowed from it, Saul, now become Paul, transformed what was then only a Jewish sect into a world-religion. That involved for him, and for all Jewish Christians, the surrender of religious convictions and rites of the Jewish faith, which had behind them undoubted divine authority, – circumcision, the strict observance of the Jewish Sabbath, the keeping of the whole law of Moses. No greater renunciation of belief, previously held as essential, has ever been made in response to a divine revelation of wider spiritual possibilities.

When he too was about the same age, Rudolf Steiner had an experience of Christ which cannot be better expressed than in his own words: "I stood before the Mystery of Golgotha in a most inward, most solemn festival of knowledge." He too was versed in the scientific and philosophic culture of his day, but also, quite uniquely, in the direct experience of the objective reality of spirit. This he saw as a divinely ordered opportunity for a great advance in the spiritual evolution of humanity, and at the heart of it – the only possibility of its realisation – a new understanding of the Deed of Christ for mankind. Like Paul, he "was not disobedient to the heavenly vision". He saw it as the divine revelation of the possibility of a great renewal of the Christ-Impulse in the life of humanity.

The acceptance of this view of the Christ of human destiny might involve the Churches in the renunciation and readaptation of some forms and beliefs that, in the evolution of Christianity in the Western world, have come to be regarded as fixed. But that renunciation would be far less than that which was involved in the birth of Christianity. The message of Anthroposophy is a challenge and an opportunity which the Christian Churches should face in the deepest seriousness.

Pietro Archiati – Reincarnation in modern life

The following quotations are taken from a publication of the same title of six lectures Pietro Archiati held in Rome in 1994.

"Reincarnation is usually considered to be an ancient, non-Christian, doctrine deriving from the East. So does it have any relevance to our time, and is it compatible with the teachings of Christianity? In a lively and fluid style, Pietro Archiati describes the approach to reincarnation taken by the spiritual master Rudolf Steiner – an approach which is wholly relevant to western consciousness and is steeped in true Christianity. ... Pietro Archiati was born in 1944 in Brescia, Italy. He studied philosophy and theology, and worked for many years as a Catholic priest. In 1977 he had a decisive encounter with the work of Rudolf Steiner. He later worked as a teacher in a seminary in South Africa. Since 1987 he has been working independently as a freelance lecturer on the scientific knowledge of the spirit inaugurated by Rudolf Steiner, which he considers essential to a regeneration of human culture."[2]

From the Preface: "I am attempting to show, in a form everyone can understand, that the awareness of reincarnation and karma is essential if Christianity is to be alive in the present and the future. – Even everyday practical life and our social contacts become at one and the same time decidedly more 'Christian' and more 'human' if we have not only a theoretical knowledge of reincarnation and karma but our heart forces live with it".

From the vantage point of his spiritual encounter with Rudolf Steiner, Archiati is reaching out to thousands of contemporaries with depth of thought and genuine understanding of the science of the spirit, as these six lectures, held in Rome in 1994 to some five hundred people from all over Italy, demonstrate.

Unlike Geddes MacGregor, Archiati is not concerned with historical arguments and theoretical reincarnation*isms*. He stands firmly in the present on the basis of Rudolf Steiner's insights and considers the beneficial effects on all walks of life, both now and

---

2 From the back cover

into the future. So we read in the sixth lecture: "In Rudolf Steiner's spiritual science Christianity is made the *basis for life* in a most real and practical way. For either daily life itself becomes Christian or there is no such thing as Christianity. True Christianity cannot exist *alongside* life, it has to be *life* itself. Essential to this living Christianity is an awareness of reincarnation and karma which in itself does not remain only a theoretical dogma but which takes such possession of our hearts that every meeting with another person becomes a Christian sacrament. Further down he says: "The Christianity of the future is the Christianity of this kind of mutual love among people who want to take into account the many past incarnations spent in the many intertwining destinies, so that a stop can be made to the judging and condemning of one another. In the Gospels Christ says, making a mark on the ground: 'Judge not, that ye be not judged'."

This is a stance which Archiati pursues in other publications in greater detail. He investigates with penetrating thoughts such virtues as *tolerance, freedom, loyalty* and more in the light of reincarnation.

In the last lecture Archiati examines the Catholic position which found expression in statements which denounce reincarnation. The International Theological Commission is given a certain official recognition within the Catholic Church. There is a document that bears the title *Current Problems of Eschatology* that appeared at the end of 1992. The ninth section of this document is about 'The Unrepeatable Nature and Uniqueness of Human Life: The Problem of Reincarnation'. The summing up of their findings appear in brackets at the end of the three relevant paragraphs: 'Denial of Hell', 'Denial of Redemption', and 'Denial of Resurrection'. With the background of his own theological studies and familiar with Rudolf Steiner's teachings on reincarnation, Archiati is emphatic in expressing his views on the content of the statements made in these documents: "These claims are outrageous if, for example, you compare them with Rudolf Steiner's understanding of reincarnation. In fact they could not possibly be more outrageous. Also everything is thrown into one basket. The 'theory of reincarnation' is referred to without mentioning which theory of reincarnation is meant. Are they speaking about Buddhism or Steiner?"

A very interesting exposition ensues but it is not my intention to enter into the depth of these questions but rather to draw the attention of the reader to a source where answers can be found. – One essential point, however, should be pointed to in Archiati's own words: "Pre-Christian religions could only speak of the soul, the astral body. So long as no "I" is there one cannot speak of reincarnation. Rudolf Steiner does not speak of metempsychosis or transmigration of the soul, meaning the passing of soul-substance from one body into another – but of reincarnation of the *spirit,* of the spiritual individuality, the human "I". Those are two totally different things. In an anthroposophical-Christian sense it is reincarnation we are talking about and not – ever! – about metempsychosis (psyche=soul)" Archiati detects in these official versions some "colossal errors of thought" and in their arguments "poor thinking, very poor thinking!" The differentiation of soul and spirit, so essential in the Christian aspect of reincarnation, also corrects the fantasy of 'thousands or millions' of reincarnations assumed by other authors, especially when taking into consideration the the in-between times spent in the worlds of spirit.

After discussing the 'Denial of the Resurrection' with the assumption of finally reaching a state forever completely independent of matter, Archiati explains: "Steiner says exactly the opposite. I understand Steiner to say the exact opposite! The point is not that human beings become 'independent' of matter, which remains the same for always, but there is a gradual transformation and spiritualisation of matter itself, this being the 'resurrection body' in the genuine Christian sense". Following this, Archiati now considers evolution at the hand of the parable of the Prodigal Son. Man was given the freedom and his share of the father's inheritance and went out into the world in order to find his own self, develop his own personality in a world of ever denser matter. He made use of an egoistic, negative freedom. This was the first part of evolution, a 'luciferic' one. With the Christ Event on earth, in Archiati's words: "The second phase of freedom is love. But the second phase cannot occur if the first one has not preceded it. In the second phase of freedom, beginning with the turning-point of evolution, the Christ Event, egoism shall be transformed into love and brought into harmony. The love of one's neighbour must be added to the love of oneself (egoism.)" This essential aspect is discussed in great detail and culminates in the following insight: "By entering into the man Jesus of Nazareth, the Christ deified human nature in an actual and total sense. Through Jesus of Nazareth, through this 'needle's eye' of the bodily structure of a single human being, the Christ entered through death, resurrection and ascension into the entire earth body in order to create the conditions necessary for the deification of man and the humanising of the whole earth. Thus we can look at the Christ Event and say that in the Christ Being we see realised all the dimensions of human evolution which have been made real through grace and freedom. In the Christ Being we already see the realisation of all those human dimesions which we, as human beings, can attain in the course of the entire second half of evolution because we have now been given the necessary possibilities – until the end of time. The 'end of time' means the end of Earth Evolution. After that there will be a kind of new beginning."

Rudolf Steiner, in one of his basic books (Esoteric Science, 1909) puts forward the vista of future phases of evolution for man and the earth.

It is astonishing how many profound aspects of a human-Christian nature Pietro Archiati was able to weave into these six lectures given in Rome of which the above digest only gives some indication. He concludes his lectures with a beautiful contemplation and image of the Rose, a flower which is deeply anchored in the soil of the earth and transforming the aspect of dark matter into light and colour of the spirit, becoming a symbol of love.

After word

During the last 86 years since Rudolf Steiner's death unparalleled changes have taken place in scientific and technological advances. These were accompanied by global concerns of climate change with the increase of natural disasters; alarming reduction of the earth's resources, including water and oil; social and political consequences with wars, producing terrorism and the break down of trust in the banking system leading to recession and unemployment. Furthermore, electronics and genetics have become a dominating factor in public and private life and the ubiquitous photographic surveillance.

The here and now is absorbing attention to a high degree so that the thought of former and future lives seems completely irrelevant. But is this the only answer? Are there not many who present questions right from birth, others who suffer illness throughout life and yet others who face sudden death or are waiting for release in death? In such situations conventional answers are often unsatisfactory and questions may arise concerning what went before birth and what destiny has in store for the individual soul and spirit after death. May the chapters of this book have stimulated own thoughts in this direction. Only if this matter becomes a heart's concern will the soil be fertile for new insights.

The author was under no illusion that this book would ever become a best-seller. Yet, because he is convinced of the truth of reincarnation and karma which he shares with increasing numbers of people he is optimistic, that the individual spirit will recognise himself as a creative and indestructible agent in the history of the world. Not just the totality of human beings presenting as an 'anthropocene' geological force now transforming the earth: but each human individuality is at work with his– or her– own transformation.

The poet, Christopher Fry, has given expression to such a change of heart and consciousness:

> The human heart can go the length of God.
> Dark and cold we may be, but this
> Is no winter now. The frozen misery
> Of centuries' breaks, cracks, begins to move;
> The thunder is the thunder of the floes,
> The thaw, the flood, the upstart Spring.
> Thank God our time is now when wrong
> Comes up to face us everywhere,
> Never to leave us till we take
> The longest stride of soul men ever took.
> Affairs are now soul size.
> The enterprise
> Is exploration into God.
> Where are you making for? It takes
> So many thousand years to wake,
>
> But will you wake for pity's sake?

We may take courage that in spite of all obstructions – a new spring is indeed arriving!

k

Translations from the German of texts by K. O. Schmidt, Thorwald Detlefson and Sigwart are by the author.

Acknowledgement

Unusually the whole of this book is an acknowledgement of the life and work of the authors referred to. They were very close to me as I entered their particular kind of being, their thoughts and intentions. Much gratitude goes to them for having shared their experiences and endeavours with a wider public.

Regarding the legalities and permission to quote from the extant literature, in several cases no longer available, I have tried to trace and contact the publishers or legal inheritors but drew blanks in most cases. My thanks therefore go to those who have responded positively. To all authors and publishers I have rendered a service by drawing attention to their publications. Every source has been acknowledged.

Much gratitude is hereby expressed to Tom Raines and Paul Carline for their valued help with proofreading and editing, also to Merrilyn Zelenka, and to Ueli Ruprecht and Rowena Ross for helping me over many computer hurdles.

Appendix A

Excerpt from 'The Riddles of Philosophy' by Rudolf Steiner

As the conclusion of his book – first published in 1901 under the title 'World and Life Conceptions in the 19th century and extended to include all major philosophies since the 6th century B.C. and published in 1914 under the title 'The Riddles of Philosophy' – Rudolf Steiner added at the end 'A Brief Outline of an Approach to Anthroposophy'. There he gives a passage on reincarnation and karma which is very helpful to a thoughtful grasp of this subject:

"The true nature of the human soul can be experienced directly if one seeks it in the character-ised way. (In the Greek era the development of the philosophical outlook led to the birth of thought. Later development led through the experience of thought to the experience of the self-conscious ego, which, although actively produced by the human soul, at the same time placed this soul in the realm of a reality that is inaccessible to the senses. Goethe stands on this ground when he strives for an idea of the plant that cannot be perceived by the senses but that contains the supersensible nature of all plants, making it possible, with the aid of this idea, to invent new plants that would have their own life.

Hegel regarded the experience of thoughts as a "standing in the true essence of the world; for him the world of thoughts became the inner essence of the world. An unbiased observation of philosophical development shows that thought experience was, to be sure, the element through which the self-conscious ego was to be placed on its own foundation. But it shows also that it is necessary to go beyond a life in mere thoughts in order to arrive at a form of inner experience that leads beyond the ordinary consciousness. ...

To Dilthey and Euken the spiritual world is a sum total of the cultural experiences of humanity. If this world is seen as the only accessible spiritual world, one does not stand on a ground firm enough to be comparable to the method of natural science. For the conception of natural science, the world is so ordered that the physical human being in his individual existence appears as a unit towards which all other natural processes and beings point. The cultural world is created by this human being. That world, however is not an individual entity of a higher nature than the individuality of the human being.

The spiritual science that the author of this book has in mind points to a form of experience that the soul can have independent from the body and in this experience an individual entity is revealed. It emerges as a higher human nature for whom the physical man is like a tool. The being that feels itself as set free, through spiritual experience, from the physical body, is a spiritual human entity that is as much at home in a spiritual world as the physical body in the physical world. . As the soul thus experiences its spiritual nature, it is also aware of the fact that it stands in a certain relation to the body. The body appears, on the one hand, as a cast of the spiritual entity; it can be compared to the shell of a snail that is like a counter-picture of the shape of the snail. On the other hand, the spirit-soul entity appears in the body like the sum total of the forces in the plant, which, after it has grown into leaf and blossom, contracts into the seed in order to prepare a new plant. One cannot experience the inner spiritual man without knowing that he contains something that will develop into a new physical man. This new human being, while living within the physical organism, has collected forces through experience that could not unfold as long as they were encased in that organism. The body has, to be sure, enabled the soul to have experiences in connection with the external world that make the inner spiritual man different from what he was before he began life in the physical body. But this body is, as it were, too rigidly organised for being transformed by the inner spiritual man according to the pattern of the new experiences. Thus there remains hidden in the human shell a spiritual being that contains the disposition of a new man.

Thoughts such as these can only be briefly indicated here. They point to a spiritual science that is essentially constructed after the model of natural science. In elaborating this spiritual science one will have to proceed more or less like the botanist when he observes a plant, the formation of its root, the growth of its stem and its leaves, and its development into blossom and fruit. In the fruit he discovers the seed of the new plant-life. As he follows the development of a plant he looks for its origin in the seed formed by the previous plant. The investigator of spiritual science will trace the process in which a human life, apart from its external manifestation, develops also an inner being.

He will find that external experiences die off like the leaves and the flowers of a plant. Within the inner being, however, he will discover a spiritual kernel, which conceals within itself the potentiality of a new life. In the infant entering life though birth he will see the return of a soul that left the world previously through the gate of death. He will learn to observe that what is handed down by heredity to the individual man from his ancestors is merely the material that is worked upon by the spiritual man in order to bring into physical existence what has been prepared seed-like in the preceding life. Seen from the viewpoint of this world conception, many facts of psychology will appear in a new light. A great number of examples could be mentioned here; it will suffice to point out only one. One can observe how the human soul is transformed by experiences that represent, in a certain sense, repetitions of earlier experiences. If somebody has read an important book in his twentieth year and reads it again in his fortieth, he experiences it as if he were a different person. If he asks without bias for the reason of this fact, he will find that what he learned from reading twenty years previous has continued to live in him and has become part of his nature. He has within him the forces that live in the book, and he finds them again when he re-reads the book at the age of forty. The same holds true with our life experiences. They become part of man himself. They live in his "ego". But it is also apparent that within the limits of one life this inner strengthening of the higher man must remain in the realm of his spirit and soul nature. Yet one can also find that this higher human being strives to become strong enough to find expression in his physical nature. The rigidity of the body prevents this from happening within a single life span. But in the central core of man there lives the potential predisposition that, together with the fruits of one life, will form a new life in the same way that the seed of a new plant lives in the plant. Moreover, it must be realised that following the entry of the soul into an independent spiritual world the results of this world are raised into consciousness in the same way that the past rises into memory. But these realities are seen as extending beyond the span of an individual life. The content of my present consciousness represents the results of my earlier physical experiences; so, too, a soul that has gone through the indicated exercises faces the whole of its physical experience and the particular configuration of its body as originating from the spirit-soul nature, whose existence preceded that of the body. This existence appears as a life in a purely spiritual world in which the soul lived before it could develop the germinal capacities of a preceding life into a new one. Only by closing one's mind to the obvious possibility that the faculties of the human soul are capable of development can one refuse to recognise the truthfulness of a person's testimony that shows that as a result of inner work one can really know of a spiritual world beyond the realm of ordinary consciousness. This knowledge leads to a spiritual apprehension of a world through which it becomes evident that the true being of the soul lies behind ordinary experiences. It also becomes clear that the soul being survives death just as the plant seed survives the decay of the plant. The insight is gained that the human soul goes through repeated lives on earth and that between these earthly lives it leads a purely spiritual existence."

It would go beyond the frame of this book to refer to the exercises referred to above, with the exception of one which is of general value. For the strengthening of memory Rudolf Steiner recommends to view in the evening the events of the day in reverse order.

Appendix B

Light Nourishment

Michael Werner – 'Life from Light' – written in collaboration with Thomas Stöckli

Magnus Magnusson: 'To me at least there is one incontrovertible conclusion – that the human mind is an infinitely more complex, mysterious and fascinating thing than we can ever imagine.'

These words are a fitting introduction to the following story, although not making reference to reincarnation and karma, it gives an impression of the human mind – or spirit – that cannot be identified with the earthly garment worn during incarnation.

Having heard of the phenomenon of Michael Werner, living without solid food for a prolonged time, the publication of the book 'Life from Light', was a welcome source of insight into this puzzling subject. The general reception is one of sensation, disbelief and scepticism; or is it a true challenge to our world-concept and scientific knowledge?

———

Preamble: In Australia in 1992, a medium by name of Jasmuheen channelled a method by which to wean oneself of the intake of ordinary nourishment and enabling a person to live on light. This is the so-called '21-day-process', which became known the world over through the book 'Living on Light' published in 1997. Her own description made up only 45 of the 200 pages; Charmaine Harley wrote the rest. The content appeared also as a leaflet with the added subtitle 'The Source of Nourishment for the New Millennium'.

—∿—

Michael Werner, a scientist with a PhD in chemistry, read the German edition of the book and, although he had certain reservations, found the core-element challenging. He knew that if experimenting it for himself, he could also stop it at any moment. He therefore went through the 21-day-process and felt motivated to carry on. Werner is a family man, and a professional and carries on with sport.

When the case came to the notice of Thomas Stöckli, a journalist, he interviewed Werner, his wife, and colleagues. They became friends and finally, together, authored the book. Stöckli encouraged Werner to subject himself to a clinical examination, which he accepted. I had the first introduction to the book when Werner faced Richard and Judy on Channel 4. I thought the conversation rather flippant, concentrating on possibly eating in secret and presenting a hoax. But by then a strict clinical examination at a Zurich hospital had already taken place.

From history only a few proven cases of living without an ordinary food intake are known: From the 15th century, Niklaus von Flüe and from the 20th century, Therese von Konersreuth. The background for both of them was religious. But in the case of Werner we have a scientist who for 15 years was an executive director of a pharmaceutical firm who subjected himself to an experiment, which could provide for our materialistic outlook, and our understanding of matter and human life, and spirit, a far-reaching challenge!

—∾—

Thomas Stöckli had to satisfy his justified scepticism by questioning Werner on many issues. Was his attitude too dogmatic and radical – presenting a danger to life? The following answer shall be given verbatim:

"For me there were points of conflict. I continued to question Werner's spiritual path, and whether, since his 'conversion', he had any specific spiritual experiences'. He answered:

"For the last 25 years I have lived intensely with anthroposophy and have worked out my own spiritual path of inner exercises. I was able to deepen my meditation and my spiritual endeavours. My deeper connection with the spiritual world did not happen automatically by renouncing physical food, but because I strive for it. One does not slip effortlessly into the spiritual. I could never be party to such a path. I am left entirely free. Neither is there any organization posing any expectations or obligations on me. I myself know of no other person practising this, except the acquaintance I have mentioned."

I kept probing: "As a scientist, how could he explain to himself the phenomenon of 'living on light'?".

Werner's answer was: "I have read everything by Rudolf Steiner concerning the process of nutrition and have found nothing that I have experienced as problematic with regard to this phenomenon, but neither have I found any explanation. The closest bridge I found was in a lecture in which Steiner said that matter is 'condensed light'. (27th May, 1910) Matter, therefore, is light and there are different ways of turning light into matter. The concept 'light' would not apply in too narrow a sense. It is the whole 'etheric' (life) environment, which we can 'inhale' with our whole sensory organization, as Steiner repeatedly explained. This could be called 'living on light'. After eating and drinking, our body breaks down the material aspect completely and it is then partly restructured and enlivened anew in order to build us up and maintain us. This helps the body to maintain its structural principles. 'Living on light' would in some senses be a simplification of this process in that the body does not require solid matter but receives its building substances and structuring forces directly from other sources. I can only say that through this phenomenon I have found an entirely new relationship to my body and earth substances. I experience it in a very inward way, yet without turning away from matter and the earth. Connected with this, however, is also an act of consciousness in that, by devotion and turning towards physical substances around me, I cultivate a conscious relationship. Otherwise, it might perhaps go astray and become a lower egotism. Even when we talk about 'living on light' we are not concerned with physical light. Light, as such, is in any case invisible. What matters is the whole energy-environment, which we may call 'ether-forces'."

—⚍—

Another quote, taken from a lecture by Werner:

"When you receive your nourishment from light, an energy or a force, or whatever you like to call it, flows into you; it is simply present when you need it. How much comes in depends on how much you use; this is like a law of nature. I do sport, for example, yet my condition is good, certainly much better than it used to be. When I say 'I live on light' people often get the wrong end of the stick. They ask: 'do you go out in the midday sun? Do you sunbathe while everyone else is having lunch?' Of course I don't and it is also entirely unnecessary. To understand what I mean by 'Light' in this context we need to define the concept more precisely. Normally when we talk of 'light' we visualize light and darkness and the variety of colours. This is inexact and is not light itself but the effect light has. Lightness and darkness and the various colours are not light but merely the effects of light. Light as such is invisible. It is everywhere, but we can only see its effects, for example, when material objects reflect parts of it, causing colours to arise. Light also exists underneath the surface of the earth, so I am sure it would also be possible to 'live on light' down there in the dark, at least for some time. So the term 'living on light' is actually misleading. It is quite simply a ubiquitous energy that is present everywhere, and one of the ways in which it reveals itself is in light. Light forms the boundary between the material and the immaterial. It also has those delicately contrasting qualities arising from its wave nature on the one hand and its particle nature on the other, its wave-particle duality. It functions on the boundary between the material and the spiritual, which is why 'living on light', does after all remain the best way of describing it. But there is more to it than 'light' and 'nourishment', so it can also be called by the name of Christ, or Allah or Krishna, or many others".

As with so many other references in this volume, these short passages are but pointers in the direction of a much more detailed and wider context.

Appendix C

Excerpt from a lecture by Rudolf Steiner

R. Steiner, from the last of four lectures, Norkoping, 16 07 1914

"… I have spoken to you of the overcoming of human egoism, and of those things we must understand before we have a right understanding of Karma. I have spoken to you of man in so far as he is not only an "I" being, but belongs to the whole Earth-existence and is thereby called to help forward the attainment of the divine aim appointed for the Earth. The Christ did not come into the world and pass through the Mystery of Golgotha in order to be something to each one of us in our egoism. It would be terrible if Christ would be so understood that the words of Paul "Not I, but Christ in me" served only to encourage a higher egoism. Christ died for the whole of humanity, for the humanity of the Earth. Christ became the central Spirit of the Earth, who has to save for the Earth the spiritual-earthly elements that flow out from man."

ISBN 0 85440 2640 0

The Author

Born in Stuttgart, Germany, in 1928, to parents devoted to the teachings of Rudolf Steiner, he attended for three years the first Waldorf (Rudolf Steiner) School, before its closure by the Nazis. He was called up with 15 years to the air home defence, later to the Labour Service. After the war he took up an agricultural apprenticeship, partly to support his elderly parents; they had lost their home during the bombing.

The training completed, he volunteered in Italian Switzerland with the care of children with special needs. This led him to his life's task, starting in 1952 with a course offered at the Camphill Rudolf Steiner Schools, Aberdeen, under the guidance of Dr Karl König.

Originally intending to return to Germany, he connected himself with this international Camphill Movement in a variety of capacities and accepted in 1971 the challenge, together with his English wife, to take on a small residential special school near Perth, in his own responsibility. Three daughters grew up there. In 1995, he was honoured with the MBE by the Queen. – After retiring in 1996 he pursued still various functions within the Camphill Movement and the local Community Council and also collated and edited 'The Lives of Camphill, An Anthology of the Pioneers' (Floris Books).

The present book is a survey of his lifelong interest and study of literature concerning karma and reincarnation and contributing thereby to a general widening of the mental horizon and preparing of a more humane and meaningful future.

Bibliography

Archiati, Pietro — *Reincarnation in modern life*, Temple Lodge, ISBN 0 904693 880

Broxham, Arnall — *More Lives than One* (see Iverson, Jeffrey)

Cerminara, Gina — *Many Mansions,* Neville Spearman Ltd 1967

Cockell, Jenny — *Yesterday's Children*, Chivers Press, Bath 1994   ISBN 0 7451 2215 9

Conacher, Douglas — *Chapters of Experience*, Frederick Muller Ltd 1973, ISBN 0584 10068 X

Dethlefsen, Thorwald — *Das Erlebnis der Wiedergeburt*, Wilhelm Goldmann Verlag 1978, ISBN3-442-11199-4

Dowding, Lord — *Letters from Men Killed in the War*, From the Web

Eisenberg, Dennis — The Express, Article Tuesday, March 28, 2000

Gershom, Yonassan — *Beyond The Ashes*, A.R.E.Press USA, ISBN 0 87604 293 0 1977

Grant, Joan — *Far Memory*, A Corgi Book 1975 – ISBN0 552 09853 1

Guirdham, Arthur — *The Cathars and Reincarnation*, NevilleSpearman Ltd 1970, ISBN 85435 290 2

Guirdham, Arthur — *We Are One Another*, Nevill Spearman Ltd 1974, ISBN 0 85207 2481

Hillringhaus, FH, Ed — *Bruecke ueber den Strom*, Verlag-Die-Kommenden 1970

Iverson, Jeffrey — *More Lives than One*, Pan Books London, ISBN 0 330 25256 9

Karlen, Barbro — *The Wolves Howled*, Clairview Books, ISBN 1 902636 18 X

Raines, Tom — *Interview with Barbro Karlen*, New View 2000/3

Kelsy, Denys	*Many Lifetimes*, A Corgi Book 1976, ISBN0 552 09942 2
Meyer, T. H.	*Rudolf Steiner's Core Mission* Temple Lodge 2010 ISBN 978 1 906999 10 0
Meyer, T. H.	*Light for a new Millennium*, ISBN 1 85584 051 0
MacGregor, Geddes	*Reincarnation in Christianity*, ISBN 0-8356-0501-9
Moodie, Dr Raymond	*Life after Life*, Bantam Books
Ritchie, George G	Return From Tomorrow, Fleming H Revell 1978, ISBN 10 8007 8412 X
Shepherd, A. P., D. D.	*The Battle for the Spirit*, Anastasi Ltd ISBN 978-0-9524403-0-7
Schmidt, K O	*Wir Leben Nicht Nur Einmal*, Drei-Eichen-Verlag 1969, München 60
Steiner, Rudolf	*An Autobiography*, Rudolf Steiner Publications, 1977 ISBN 0 8334 3501 9
Steiner, Rudolf	*Reincarnation and Karma*, Anthroposophic Press 1977, ISBN 0 88010 366 3
Stevenson, Dr Ian	*The Pioneer of Reincarnation*, http://www.near-death.com/Research/experiences/reincarnation01.htm
Wambach, Dr. Helen	*Life Before Life*, Bantam Books ISBN, 0 553 12450 1
Werner/Stöckli	*Life from Light*, Clairview Books, ISBN 978 1905570 05 8
Whitton / Fisher	*Life Between Life*, Grafton Books / Collins, 1986, ISBN 0 586 07091 5
Woodward, Bob	*Spirit Communications*, Athena Press 2007, ISBN 1 84401 959 4
Woolger, Roger PhD	Other Lives, Other Selves, Dolphin/Doubleday, Inc., New York 1987, ISBN 1 85274 084 1

Lightning Source UK Ltd.
Milton Keynes UK
UKOW020307061111

181582UK00001B/1/P